Teaching and Le[arning]
Key Stage _
Numeracy Activity Book

Mental Mathematics 2: Multiplication and Division

Hilary Koll
and Steve Mills

Letts
EDUCATIONAL

Every effort has been made to trace ~~~~~~~~~~ers and to obtain their permission for the use of copyright material. The authors and publishers will gladly receive information enabling them to rectify any error or omission in subsequent editions.

First published 1999

Letts Educational, Schools and Colleges Division, 9–15 Aldine Street,
London W12 8AW
Tel: 0181 740 2270
Fax: 0181 740 2280

Text © Hilary Koll and Steve Mills
Designed, produced and edited by Gecko Limited, Bicester, Oxon
Illustrations © Chris Rothero and Harvey Collins

All our rights reserved. No part of this publication may be reproduced, stored in a retrieval system, or transmitted, in any form or by any means, electronic, mechanical, photocopying, recording or otherwise, without prior permission of Letts Educational.

British Library Cataloguing-in-Publication Data
A CIP record for this book is available from the British Library

ISBN 1 84085 182 1
Printed in Great Britain by Ashford Colour Press
Letts Educational is the trading name of BPP [Letts Educational] Ltd

Contents

How to use this book 4

PART I — COMPETENCIES FOR MULTIPLICATION AND DIVISION 6

1. Understands multiplication and division as inverses and understands commutativity, associativity and distributivity 6
2. Can count forwards and backwards in 1s, 2s, 5s, 10s, 100s, 1000s, from any number 7
3. Can read, write and order numbers to 100, to 1000 and beyond 8
4. Can instantly recall all tables facts up to 10 × 10 and division facts as reversed tables facts, doubles of numbers to 20, 50, 100, doubles of multiples of 10 and can recognise multiples of 2, 5, 10, 100 9
5. Understands place value ideas and can partition numbers, and understands relationships between single- and 2- or 3-digit numbers 11

PART II — MULTIPLICATION 15

Children should check answers using division and approximate using repeated addition.

6. Can multiply a 2-digit number by a single digit mentally 15
7. Can multiply any number by 10 mentally 17
8. Can multiply any number by 9 or 11 mentally 20
9. Can multiply any number by 100 mentally 24
10. Can multiply any number by 99 or 101, etc. mentally 27
11. Can multiply any number by 1000 mentally 29
12. Can multiply any number by 999 or 1001, etc. mentally 33
13. Can multiply two multiples of 10, 100, 1000* mentally 36
14. Can multiply a near multiple of 10, 100, 1000* by a multiple of 10, 100, 1000 mentally 39
15. Can multiply any 2-digit number by a multiple of 10, 100, 1000* mentally 41
16. Can multiply a decimal (1 decimal place) by a single digit mentally 44

PART III — DIVISION 46

Children should check answers using multiplication and approximate using repeated subtraction.

17. Can divide a 2-digit number by a single digit without or with remainders mentally 46
18. Can divide a multiple of 10 by 10, and a multiple of 100 by 10 or 100 mentally 49
19. Can divide any number by 10, 100, 1000 mentally 51
20. Can divide a multiple of 100, 1000* by a multiple of 10, 100* mentally 54
21. Can divide a single digit by a larger single digit giving a fractional or decimal answer mentally 56

*Where multiples do not contain more than 1 non-zero digit, for example, 500 is fine, 530 is not

R. Resource sheets 58

A. Answers 61

How to use this book

Mathematics is, for many children, the most difficult subject to learn in school. For many teachers it is a difficult subject to teach well. Why is this? One reason is that mathematics is a hierarchical subject, that is, it's arranged in such a way that certain things need to be understood before much sense can be made of later work. Numbers to 10 need to be understood before we teach numbers to 100, for example.

This is in contrast to most other parts of the primary school curriculum which are less hierarchically arranged. It's possible to know about the Ancient Greeks without knowing anything about the Aztecs, and to understand weather but not settlement. Each one doesn't depend on the other having been understood. Mathematics is not like that: it's like a spy thriller on television with lots of episodes. Miss one and it's difficult to make sense of the rest.

Because of this it is important that we, as teachers of mathematics, have a clear sense of progression within the area of mathematics we are teaching. This helps us to become aware of which episodes children might have missed along the way, and therefore where they are in their understanding. Similarly, it ensures that activities have a clear progression to help children build on to the knowledge and understanding they already have.

This book provides activities for teaching mental strategies for multiplication and division and is part of a series of eleven books designed to be used alongside the *Teacher's Assessment Book* of this *Key Stage 2 Numeracy Pack*. The *Teacher's Assessment Book* contains *detailed progressions* and *photocopiable diagnostic assessments* for place value, addition, subtraction, multiplication, division, fractions, decimals, percentages, number patterns/algebra and mental mathematics.

The detailed progression and diagnostic test for mental strategies for multiplication and division in the *Teacher's Assessment Book* will help you to determine the level of children's knowledge and understanding. The test will show where on the progression children are and, therefore, which of the activities might be most appropriate. The activities are divided into sections which correspond to the statements in the teaching progression. Each activity has a specific purpose in relation to this progression. There are activities for *whole-class* use, perhaps as a 10–15-minute introduction, for smaller *group* work and for *individual* work. Each activity has a code which shows how it might be best used.

Summary of codes for the different types of activities/lesson ideas

This symbol indicates that the activity can be used for whole-class or large-group interactive work. Children will usually be required to sit facing a board or flipchart and the teacher will be expected to lead the discussion/activity. Inclusion of all children in the interactive work will be necessary through questioning and giving examples at a variety of levels for different children. Approximate times are given for these activities.

This symbol indicates that the activity can be used for group work. This might be an activity on a photocopiable worksheet or one which the teacher introduces verbally to a group. The children can then take this to their 'table' and work cooperatively. There will be times where the teacher is required to support a group in their work and other times when children can work independently. The length of these activities will vary according to the children's abilities.

This symbol indicates that the activity can be used for individual practice and consolidation work. This might take the form of a photocopiable worksheet or an activity that the teacher can introduce verbally and children can take away to do on their own.

Resources

Most material required for these activities – such as number lines, hundred squares and photocopiable number cards – is included in this book. For some of these activities, however, base 10 material (sometimes called Dienes blocks or hundreds, tens and units) will be required.

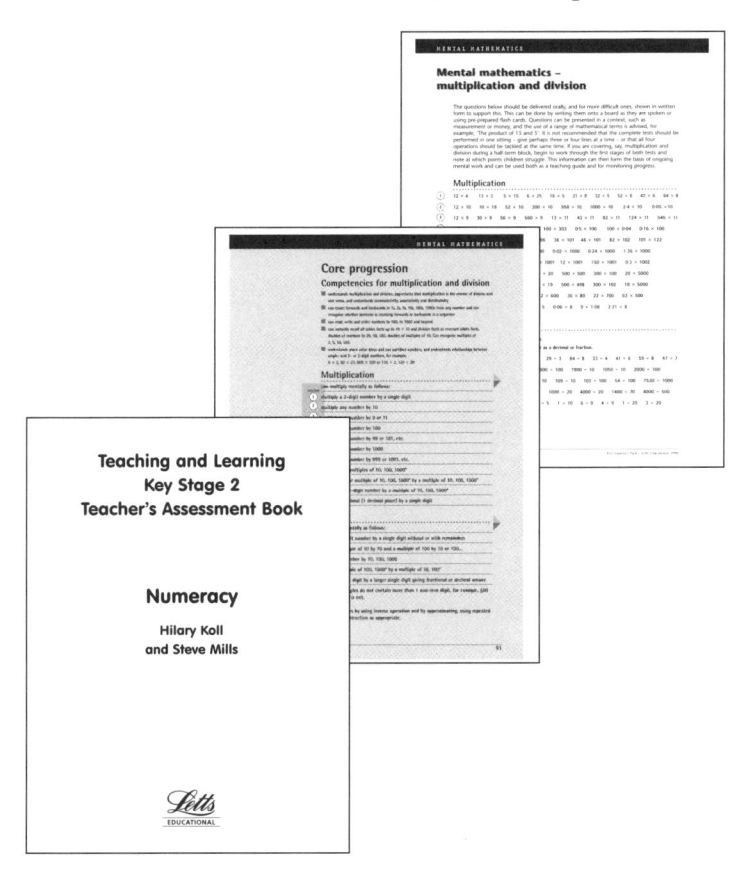

PART I COMPETENCIES FOR MULTIPLICATION AND DIVISION

① Understands multiplication and division as inverses and understands commutativity, associativity and distributivity

ACTIVITY 1.1

Resources
- 'Connect 4!' game board on page 12
- 2 colours of cubes or counters
- a calculator

Connect 4!

This is a game for two players. Children take turns to choose a number in the grid and to work out mentally how many sixes make that number. (The grid also allows the game to be played using twos or threes if appropriate.) If the player is correct they can cover that number with a cube or counter in their colour. Calculators can be used to check answers. Four cubes or counters in a line win the game.

Encourage children to think of both multiplication and division, by thinking of 24 as 4×6 and $24 \div 6 = 4$, etc.

ACTIVITY 1.2

Resources
- none

Meet Rosie and Jim

Meet Rosie and Jim. Rosie is a sweet, helpful girl. Jim is more mischievous. He always undoes whatever Rosie does, by performing the inverse operation to Rosie. Draw Rosie and Jim on the board. Put a column of numbers, 1–10, to the left of Rosie. Write a multiplication instruction in the first box beneath Rosie, as shown.

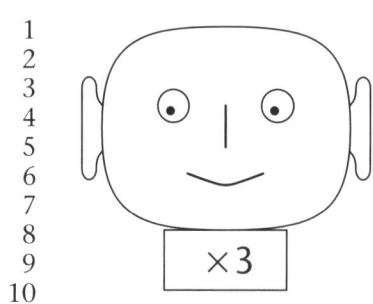

```
1
2
3
4
5
6
7
8
9
10
```
          $\times 3$

Ask children to help Rosie to take the first number, apply the rule in the box beneath, and produce a number on the right. This number is now fed to Jim, whose rule is the inverse of Rosie's. So, if Rosie's rule is $\times 3$, Jim's is $\div 3$. Eventually we will produce, to the right of Jim, the same list of numbers that we began with, as shown below. Emphasise that Jim always undoes whatever Rosie does.

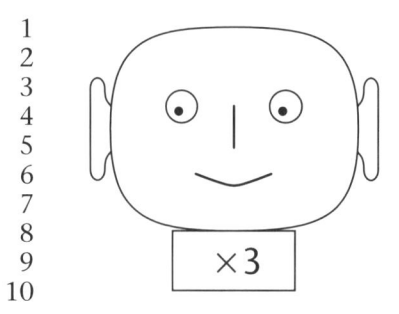

```
1        3         1
2        6         2
3        9         3
4       12         4
5       15         5
6       18         6
7       21         7
8       24         8
9   ×3  27    ÷3   9
10       30        10
```

ACTIVITY 1.3

Resources
- 'Working out' sheet on page 13

Working out

This activity allows children to 'create' and 'undo' number statements using multiplication and division as inverse operations.

6

PART I COMPETENCIES FOR MULTIPLICATION AND DIVISION

2. Can count forwards or backwards in 1s, 2s, 5s, 10s, 100s, 1000s, from any number

Activity 2.1

Resources
- 0–100 number line is useful

Long jumping

Ask the children to count on or back from a given number in different-sized steps, for example, forwards in ones from 34, backwards in ones from 43. You may be surprised at how difficult some of them find it.

Repeat the instructions, but ask them to count on or back in tens from a given number, for example, backwards in tens from 72, forwards in tens from 23.

Repeat the instructions for jumps of different sizes.

If children can be arranged in a circle, turns can be taken to give the next number.

If you have children who are experiencing difficulty, it is important that a number line with numbers from 0 to 100 is on display.

Activity 2.2

Resources
- none

Scarf steps

Draw a striped scarf like the one below on the board. Give a start and finish number in the end sections (ensuring that there are the correct number of sections) and ask children to come up and write the numbers in order between the given numbers. For example,

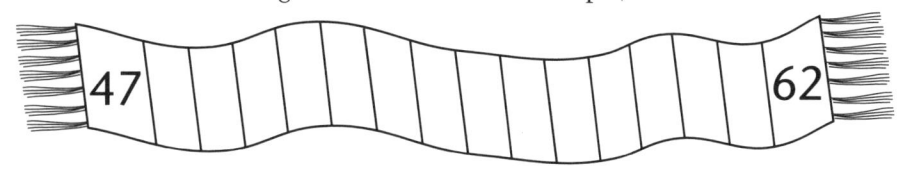

47 ... 62

Activity 2.3

Resources
- none

Following the path

Draw a length of pavement on the board, as shown. Choose a 2-digit number and write it into the first segment. Ask the children to add 10 to the number and write it in the next segment. Continue adding ten and putting the new number into the next section until the path is filled.

Write +8 underneath the path and ask the children to add 8 to the first number in the path, making 24 in this case. Write this answer onto the second path, as below.

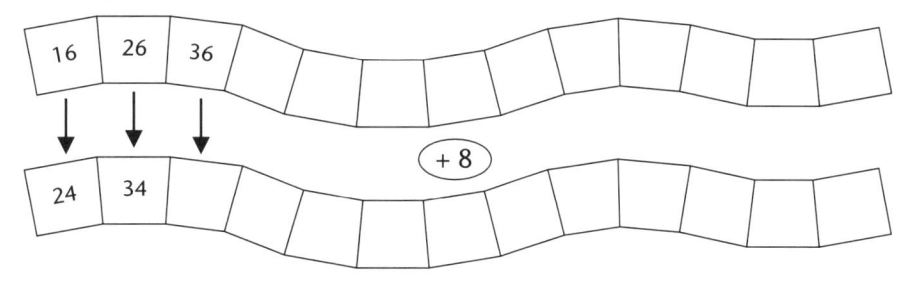

16 26 36
↓   ↓   ↓   +8
24 34

Continue to add 8 to each of the numbers in the first path and write the answer in the second path. What do the children notice about the numbers? Why does this happen? Use a number line to demonstrate that numbers follow similar patterns, going up in tens.

Repeat this activity, beginning with a different number and with a new number to add. Try adding 100 or 1000 to each successive number on the path.

PART I   COMPETENCIES FOR MULTIPLICATION AND DIVISION

(3) Can read, write and order numbers to 100, to 1000 and beyond

See the Place Value Teaching and Learning Activity Book *in this series for more ideas.*

ACTIVITY 3.1
Resources
- none

Things in common
Draw a 4 × 4 grid. Put in any numbers to 999 randomly, as shown.

266	765	305	969
929	602	362	324
799	977	325	528
194	747	594	922

Ask the children questions which involve them looking at the separate parts of each number, that is, hundreds, tens and units. Here are some examples.

- What do these numbers have in common, 266, 765, 969?
- Can you find any numbers that have 2 in the tens column?
- Can you find three other numbers that have something in common?
- Which numbers have the smallest units digit?
- Which number/s have the largest hundreds digit?
- Can you put these numbers in order of size …?

ACTIVITY 3.2
Resources
- none

Passing it on
This is an activity for groups of three children. The first child writes a number on a piece of paper, for example, 471 or 3062. The paper is given to a second child who reads it and tells a third child who writes the number down. The resulting number is then compared with the original number. Groups can score points for each correct result.

ACTIVITY 3.3
Resources
- none

Whose turn to order?
Write four digits on the board, as shown.

| 3 | 9 | 7 | 6 |

Ask the children to list all the 4-digit numbers that can be made from these digits in their books. How many can each group find? (There are 24 in total.) Get each group to say the numbers and list them on the board. Now ask the groups to write them in ascending order in their books. Discuss the correct order as a whole class once the groups have agreed on their order.

This can be differentiated by using 3 or 5 digits for different groups. Be aware, however, that whilst only 6 numbers can be made from 3 digits, 120 can be made from 5!

8

PART I   COMPETENCIES FOR MULTIPLICATION AND DIVISION

④ Can instantly recall all tables facts up to 10 × 10 and division facts as reversed tables facts, doubles of numbers to 20, 50, 100, doubles of multiples of 10 and can recognise multiples of 2, 5, 10, 100

ACTIVITY 4.1

Resources
- none

Splash!

On the board, draw a river with some stepping stones as shown below. Put a single-digit number in each stone, in random order. For example,

7 | 2 8 0 6 7 1
Start   Finish

Choose a number, for example, 7. Ask children in turn to take a step across the river, by multiplying the start number, 7, by a number on a stone. Anyone getting an answer wrong falls in, resulting in a 'Splash!'. In this example children would answer 14, 56, 0, 42, 49, 7 and finish.

Use a similar activity to practise division facts, as shown. (Numbers on the stones are divided by the start number.)

7 | 42 28 70 56 49 63
Start   Finish

ACTIVITY 4.2

Resources
- children will need their books or a piece of squared paper

Bingo

Ask the children to draw a 4 × 3 grid and to write a number between 0 and 30 in each section of the grid. All the numbers should be different. For example,

5	18	21	6
0	15	30	14
19	27	10	22

While they are doing this note down all the numbers from 0 to 30 in a column on the left of a piece of paper (the back of a diary or mark book is a useful place, so that it can be used regularly).

Call out calculations, for example, 3 × 6 or 27 ÷ 3 and note them down. Emphasise multiplication and division wherever possible, for example, creating 19 from 6 × 3 + 1 and 13 from 39 ÷ 3. If children have the answer on their grid they cross it out. The first person to cross out all their numbers accurately wins. However, it is worth continuing to call out numbers until a calculation has been given for all of them. Some children may still have numbers remaining. If you have noted down the calculations given for each number then errors can be identified and children can be encouraged to learn particular facts that they do not know.

PART I COMPETENCIES FOR MULTIPLICATION AND DIVISION

ACTIVITY 4.3

Resources
- none

Turning the tables

On the board, write some tables facts such as 6 × 3 = 18, 2 × 7 = 14, 6 × 5 = 30.

Ask children to 'turn the tables' and rewrite these as division facts.

Write up this 'tables fact' △ × ◯ = ▭
and ask someone to rewrite this!

Assuming these shapes stand for whole numbers, which of these 'numbers' is the largest (the rectangle)?

In division statements made with whole numbers the largest number is always the first number. This can help children when rearranging tables facts.

Begin to ask division questions that are reversed tables facts, for example, 24 ÷ 6 = ? Children can be put into teams to answer and points scored for correct answers.

In the same way that tables facts are tested, division facts are also important.

ACTIVITY 4.4

Resources
- none, although a dartboard is useful

Doubling darts

Draw a basic dartboard on the board with the numbers arranged clockwise, from the top, in ascending order, as shown. Ask the class to count round the board together. Now point out the double ring and ask what the value of a dart landing in double 1, double 2, would be, etc., until the children are counting round the board in doubles. What do they notice about all the doubles? Why are they always even?

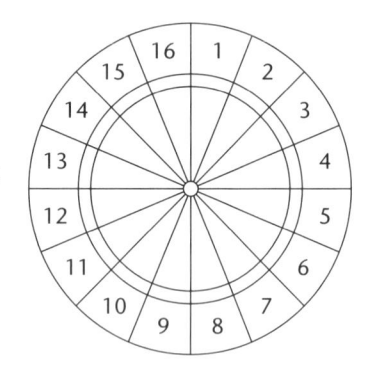

Now ask the children to give you the doubles of selected numbers chosen at random. You can introduce a board with a random number arrangement – a real dartboard is ideal. 'Alien' dartboards can be developed, using numbers from 21 to 40, for example, and beyond.

ACTIVITY 4.5

Resources
- calculators

Constant function

Using the constant function facility on a calculator is a useful way of generating multiples. Ask children to explore the patterns produced by pressing these buttons.

2 + + = = = = = = = =..., 5 + + = = = = = = = =...,
10 + + = = = = = = = =..., 100 + + = = = = = = = =...

They will soon realise that they have made a 'tables' machine. Ask them to list the multiples vertically and, next to each one, to write the table fact that would generate it. Encourage them to explore the patterns produced on a number line and to describe the sequences produced in words. For example, 'it goes up one hundredth each time, starting at 9 hundredths to begin with. 0·09 plus one hundredth equals 0·1..., etc.'.

PART I COMPETENCIES FOR MULTIPLICATION AND DIVISION

5) Understands place value ideas and can partition numbers, and understands relationships between single- and 2- or 3-digit numbers

See the Place Value Teaching and Learning Activity Book *in this series for more ideas.*

ACTIVITY 5.1

Resources
- none

Grids

Draw a 4 × 4 grid, put in any numbers to 100 or 1000 randomly, for example,

34	124	218	40
162	43	824	201
241	200	305	87
64	109	388	741

This grid can be used for asking questions, such as the following.

- 'How many numbers can you see with 2 units?'
- 'Which numbers are between 10 and 100?'
- 'Which numbers are between 100 and 500?'
- 'Which numbers have 4 in the tens column?'
- 'Which numbers have the same number of tens as units?'
- 'Which number is exactly 500 more than another number?'
- 'Which number is half of another number?'
- 'Find a route from side to side, or top to bottom, where the units digits are less than 5.'
- 'Find a route where the tens digits are less than 4.'

Encourage children to partition the numbers into their hundreds, tens and units parts, for example,

$$824 = 800 + 20 + 4 \text{ or } 8 \text{ hundreds, 2 tens and 4 units, etc.}$$

ACTIVITY 5.2

Resources
- 'Spot the pattern!' sheet on page 14
- calculator

Spot the pattern!

This activity provides children with an opportunity to explore the 'moving digits' when a number is multiplied by 10 or 100, so that they begin to appreciate the relationships between these numbers. A calculator can be used for checking.

PART I COMPETENCIES FOR MULTIPLICATION AND DIVISION

Connect 4!

Take turns to choose a number from the grid.
Work out in your head how many sixes will make the number.
Ask your opponent to check your answer on the calculator.
If you are right cover the number with a cube or counter.
The first player to get 4 cubes in a line is the winner.
The winning line can be across, down or diagonal.

6	0	24	18	12
36	18	48	6	30
24	36	42	12	24
48	30	54	0	42
6	18	60	36	30

PART I COMPETENCIES FOR MULTIPLICATION AND DIVISION

1.3

Name ....

Working out

Use these 4 numbers only. **6** **9** **5** **8**

Write one of the numbers in each square to make each statement correct.

(1) ☐ × ☐ = 30   (2) ☐ = 30 ÷ ☐

(3) ☐ × ☐ = 40   (4) ☐ = 40 ÷ ☐

(5) ☐ × ☐ = 45   (6) ☐ = 45 ÷ ☐

(7) ☐ × ☐ = 48   (8) ☐ = 48 ÷ ☐

Now try these.

(9) ☐ = 54 ÷ ☐   (10) ☐ × ☐ = 54

(11) ☐ = 72 ÷ ☐   (12) ☐ × ☐ = 72

Change!

Change your numbers to these. **3** **4** **7** **9**

Use these numbers to complete these statements.

(13) ☐ × ☐ = 12   (14) ☐ = 27 ÷ ☐

(15) ☐ × ☐ = 63   (16) ☐ = 28 ÷ ☐

(17) ☐ × ☐ = 21   (18) ☐ = 63 ÷ ☐

(19) ☐ × ☐ = 36   (20) ☐ = 36 ÷ ☐

KS2 Numeracy Pack © Letts Educational, 1999   13

PART I COMPETENCIES FOR MULTIPLICATION AND DIVISION

5.2

Name ....

Spot the pattern!

(1) Try these questions and use a calculator to check your answers.

Th H T U	Th H T U	Th H T U
4 × 1 =	4 × 2 =	4 × 4 =
4 × 10 =	4 × 20 =	4 × 40 =
4 × 100 =	4 × 200 =	4 × 400 =

What do you notice about each set of answers? ....

....

(2) Try these.

Th H T U	Th H T U	Th H T U
4 × 1 =	4 × 2 =	4 × 4 =
40 × 1 =	40 × 2 =	40 × 4 =
400 × 1 =	400 × 2 =	400 × 4 =

Does the same pattern of answers appear? ....

Why? ....

(3) Try these.

Th H T U	Th H T U	Th H T U
5 × 4 =	3 × 7 =	4 × 9 =
50 × 40 =	30 × 70 =	40 × 90 =

What happens with these sets of questions? ....

....

(4) Work out the answers to these questions without a calculator.

2 × 8 =	20 × 8 =	200 × 8 =	80 × 2 =	20 × 80 =
4 × 3 =	40 × 3 =	400 × 3 =	30 × 4 =	40 × 30 =
5 × 9 =	50 × 9 =	500 × 9 =	90 × 5 =	50 × 90 =
7 × 4 =	70 × 4 =	700 × 4 =	40 × 7 =	70 × 40 =
12 000 ÷ 3 =	1200 ÷ 3 =	120 ÷ 3 =		12 ÷ 3 =
32 000 ÷ 4 =	3200 ÷ 4 =	320 ÷ 4 =		32 ÷ 4 =

6 Can multiply a 2-digit number by a single digit mentally

For example, 12 × 4, 13 × 3, 5 × 15, 6 × 25, 64 × 8

ACTIVITY 6.1

Resources
- none

Rays of hope

Draw a diagram on the board like the one shown. Ask children to suggest multiplication facts that make the number in the sun. Write each one at the end of one of the sun's rays. Encourage commutativity by 'turning the tables' to emphasise that the order does not matter.

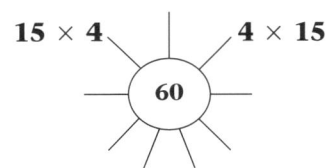

15 × 4   4 × 15
60

ACTIVITY 6.2

Resources
- none

Sun factors

Draw a diagram on the board like the one shown. Ask children to suggest factors of the number in the sun. Write each one at the end of one of the rays. Draw attention to the fact that all numbers have an even number of factors, unless they are square numbers. All square numbers have an odd number of factors.

The multiplicative aspect can be emphasised by encouraging children to write the pairs of factors at the ends of opposite rays.

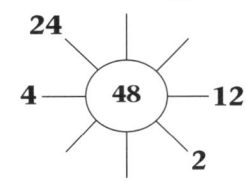

24
4 — 48 — 12
2

ACTIVITY 6.3

Resources
- packs of playing cards or sets of number cards with 4 each of the numbers 1–5

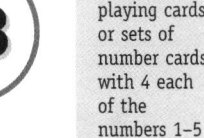

What a turn up!

This is an activity for pairs of children. Remove all the cards above 5 from the playing cards. Children shuffle the cards and place them face down. Player 1 turns up three cards. The first two cards create a tens and units number with the third card providing a number to multiply by. For example, the cards on the left create the calculation 42 × 3.

Player 1 answers the question and scores a point for a correct answer. Player 2 then has a turn. The winner is the first to reach 11 points. A calculator can be used to settle any disputes. As the children's mental skills improve, further cards can be added to the pack, until all the cards from aces to tens are included. As an alternative, a set of three dice can provide the basis for the activity with numbers 1–6.

ACTIVITY 6.4

Resources
- 'How many times?' sheet on page 16
- three dice
- two colours of cubes or counters

How many times?

This is a game for pairs of children. Players take turns to roll three dice. Players choose two of the numbers to create a tens and units number with the third dice providing a number to multiply by. The dice shown on the left could create the calculations 32 × 4, 23 × 4, 42 × 3, 24 × 3, etc.

Having done their calculation, each player looks to see whether their answer appears on the grid on the sheet. If it does they place a counter of their colour on it. The winner is the first player to get five counters on the grid. Should this prove too easy, a line of three in any direction can be the target.

15

PART II   MULTIPLICATION

How many times?

Roll 3 dice. Choose 2 of the numbers to be a tens and units number. Multiply this number by the third number. If the answer is in the grid, put a counter on it. The winner is the first player to get 5 counters on the grid.

12	42	36	260
172	25	88	129
72	96	125	144
33	66	140	84
90	68	255	258
86	16	115	396
212	153	122	123
168	48	46	62
155	44	140	78

7 Can multiply any number by 10 mentally

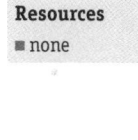

For example, 12 × 10, 10 × 19, 52 × 10, 300 × 10, 958 × 10, 2·4 × 10

ACTIVITY 7.1

Resources
- none

T	U	
	7	×10
7	0	

Moving digits

Draw tens and units columns on the board as shown on the left.

Ask children for a single-digit number, for example, 7. Write it in the units column. Ask children for the answer when this is multiplied by 10. Write down this answer. Continue this process, noting down all the numbers beneath each other in the correct columns, as shown.

T	U	
	7	×10
7	0	
	6	×10
6	0	
	9	×10
9	0	etc.

Draw children's attention to what is happening to the digits when we multiply by 10, *i.e. they move one place to the left and a 0 fills the space left behind.* This helps to avoid the 'add a nought' which causes difficulties when decimals are encountered.

ACTIVITY 7.2

Resources
- 'Machine madness!' sheet on page 18

Machine madness!

This function machine activity offers children the opportunity to practise multiplying by 10.

ACTIVITY 7.3

Resources
- 'Birthday treats!' sheet on page 19

Birthday treats!

This activity is set in the context of 'Big Ben's Burgers' and involves children in calculating the cost of 10 lots of various items.

ACTIVITY 7.4

Resources
- resource sheet 1: number generator on page 58

Number generator

Use resource sheet 1: number generator on page 58 to create oral multiplication and division questions. Select randomly from the sheet and generate questions such as 'What is ... multiplied by 10?'. Use the range of terms which indicate multiplication, including 'product', 'lots of', 'multiplied by', 'times', 'groups of', etc. and those that indicate division, such as 'divided by', 'shared between', etc. Set questions in a context, for example, 'An item costs £..., how much will 10 of them cost?' or 'My journey to work is 5·2 km. How far do I travel in one week if I go there and back 5 times?'.

PART II MULTIPLICATION

7.2

Name ....

Machine madness!

Help! All our machines are going wrong. Help us by filling in the blanks.

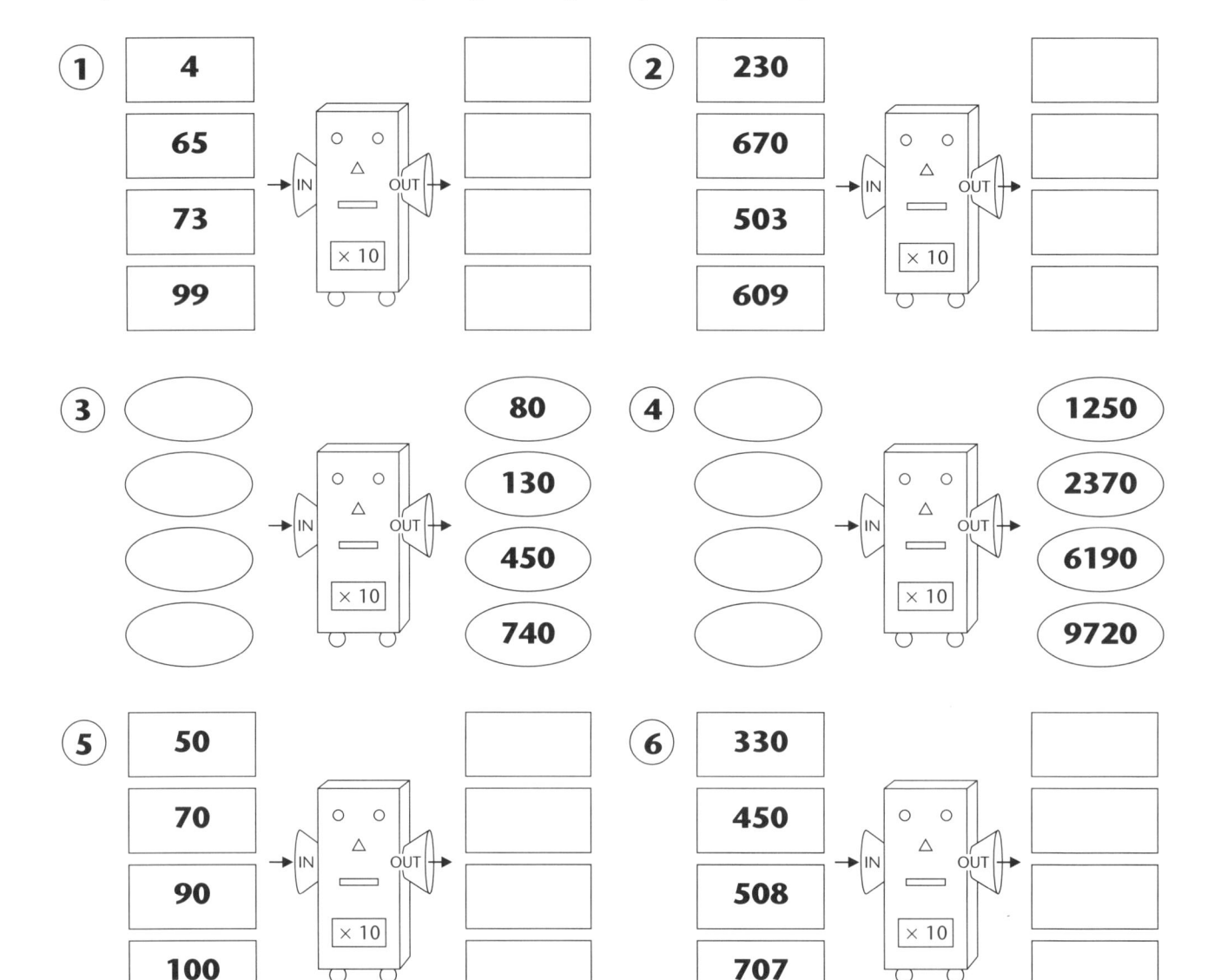

1) IN: 4, 65, 73, 99 → ×10 → OUT: ___, ___, ___, ___

2) IN: 230, 670, 503, 609 → ×10 → OUT: ___, ___, ___, ___

3) IN: ___, ___, ___, ___ → ×10 → OUT: 80, 130, 450, 740

4) IN: ___, ___, ___, ___ → ×10 → OUT: 1250, 2370, 6190, 9720

5) IN: 50, 70, 90, 100 → ×10 → OUT: ___, ___, ___, ___

6) IN: 330, 450, 508, 707 → ×10 → OUT: ___, ___, ___, ___

7) Choose some numbers of your own for this machine.

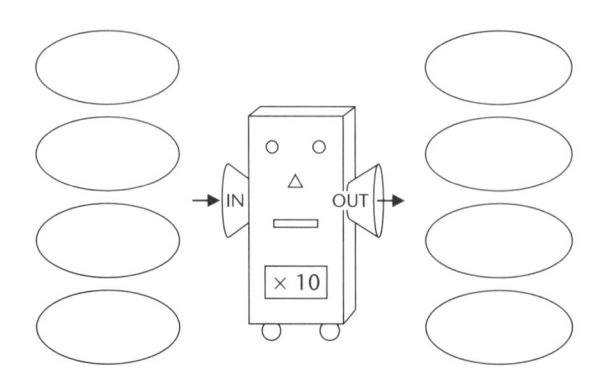

7 CAN MULTIPLY ANY NUMBER BY 10 MENTALLY

7.3

Name ....

Birthday treats!

It's Molly and Jack's birthday. They are off to Big Ben's Burgers with some of their friends.

Look at the price list.

Prices	
Big Ben	99p
Orange juice	50p
Fries	75p
Milk shake	£1.12
Apple pie	67p
Ice-cream	£1.25
Coffee	80p
Milk	46p
Tea	75p

(1) What is the most expensive thing they can buy?

....

(2) What is the cheapest? ....

If you're working out how much your food will cost it is sometimes useful to 'round' the numbers up or down, like this.
Instead of 2 Big Bens at 99p, pretend it's 2 Big Bens at £1 each and then take away 2 lots of 1p at the end!
2 × £1 = £2   £2 – 2p = £1.98

Molly and Jack have invited 4 friends each to Big Ben's.

(3) How many children is that altogether? ....

(4) If the children all wanted a Big Ben how much would that cost? ....
(You could say 10 × £1 and then take away 10 lots of 1p at the end.)

(5) How much would 10 milk shakes cost? ....

(6) What about 10 teas? ....

(7) A 'Smily Meal' costs £2.70 and contains a Big Ben, milk shake and fries.

How much would 10 Smily Meals cost? ....

(8) What have you noticed about what happens when you multiply a number by 10? ....

How quickly can you answer these questions?

(9) 10 apple pies cost ....

(10) 10 milks cost ....

(11) 10 orange juices cost ....

(12) How many ice-creams were bought for £12.50? ....

(13) How many bags of fries were bought for £7.50? ....

(14) Which things would you choose for your meal? ....

....

How much would ten of your meals cost? ....

KS2 Numeracy Pack © Letts Educational, 1999

PART II   MULTIPLICATION

8) Can multiply any number by 9 or 11 mentally

For example, 12 × 9, 30 × 9, 560 × 9, 13 × 11, 43 × 11, 11 × 124

ACTIVITY 8.1

Resources
- none

Elevenses

Once children are comfortable with multiplying by 10, they can use this skill as the basis for multiplying by 9 and 11. Ask children to multiply by 10, for example, 15 × 10, 23 × 10, etc. Now develop these, as below.

$$15 \times 10 = 150 \quad \text{so} \quad 15 \times 11 = 15 \times 10 + 15 \times 1$$

This can be shortened to $\quad 15 \times 11 = 15 \times 10 + 15 \quad$ as soon as the children understand what is happening.

Ask them to solve further calculations in the same way, emphasising the strategy involved.

ACTIVITY 8.2

Resources
- none

And now to nines ...

Activity 8.1, *'Elevenses'* can naturally be used to develop competence in multiplying by nine. Once again reiterate multiplying by ten and then subtract one lot of the number being multiplied.

$$23 \times 10 = 230 \quad \text{so} \quad 23 \times 9 = 23 \times 10 - 23 \times 1$$

As above, this can quickly become $\quad 23 \times 9 = 23 \times 10 - 23.$

ACTIVITY 8.3

Resources
- 'Doing the shopping' sheet on page 21

Doing the shopping

This sheet provides opportunity for children to practise and consolidate multiplying by 11 and 9 in the context of money. Later questions extend this by asking children to find multiples of 11 and 9 by doubling.

ACTIVITY 8.4

Resources
- 'More birthday treats!' sheet on page 22

More birthday treats!

This sheet develops Activity 7.3, *'Birthday treats!'* on page 17, to include multiplication by 11 and 9.

ACTIVITY 8.5

Resources
- 'Circuit training! cards' on page 23

Circuit training!

Give one card to each child and read the question on one card aloud, for example, '13 × 11 = ...?'. One child in the group will have a card which has the answer to the question, which they call out, followed by the question on their card. Play continues until the answer on the original card is reached.

8 CAN MULTIPLY ANY NUMBER BY 9 OR 11 MENTALLY

8.3

Name ....

Doing the shopping

Find the missing prices by using the information given.

1 1 chocolate bar costs 32p. What is the cost of:

11 bars? .... 9 bars? ....

2 1 magazine costs £1.75. What is the cost of:

11 magazines? .... 9 magazines? ....

3 1 can of cola costs 42p. What is the cost of:

11 cans? .... 9 cans? ....

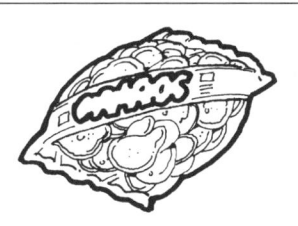

4 1 packet of crisps costs 37p. How much are:

11 packets? .... 9 packets? ....

5 A Big Ben's Burger costs 99p. How much are:

11 burgers? .... 9 burgers? ....

22 burgers? .... 18 burgers? ....

6 At Big Ben's a bag of fries costs 75p. How much are:

11 bags? .... 9 bags? ....

22 bags? .... 18 bags? ....

KS2 Numeracy Pack © Letts Educational, 1999

PART II   MULTIPLICATION

8.4

Name ....

More birthday treats!

It's Pauline and Iain's birthday. They are off to Big Ben's Burgers with some of their friends.

Look at the price list.

Prices	
Big Ben	99p
Fries	78p
Milk shake	£1.16
Apple pie	69p
Ice-cream	£1.30
Coffee	80p
Milk	46p
Orange juice	50p

(1) What is the most expensive thing they can buy?
....

(2) What is the cheapest? ....

Pauline and Iain have invited 9 friends to Big Ben's, making 11 altogether.

(3) If all the children wanted a Big Ben how much would that cost? ....

(4) How much would it cost if Pauline and Iain didn't have Big Ben's? ....

(5) How much would 11 milk shakes cost? ....

(6) How much would 9 milk shakes cost? ....

(7) How much would 11 bags of fries cost? ....

(8) Pauline and Iain still aren't hungry, so how much for 9 bags of fries? ....

(9) A 'Smily Meal', which contains a Big Ben, milkshake and fries, costs £2.75.

How much would 11 Smily Meals cost? ....

How much would 9 Smily Meals cost? ....

How quickly can you answer these?

(10) 11 apple pies cost ....

(11) 9 milks cost ....

(12) 11 orange juices cost ....

(13) How many ice-creams were bought for £14.30? ....

(14) Which things would you choose for your meal? ....

....

How much would 11 of your meals cost? ....

Circuit training! cards

99	143	108	144
13 × 11 =	9 × 12 =	16 × 9 =	11 × 15 =
165	**220**	**72**	**216**
20 × 11 =	8 × 9 =	9 × 24 =	11 × 12 =
132	**275**	**279**	**405**
25 × 11 =	9 × 31 =	45 × 9 =	11 × 36 =
396	**572**	**162**	**342**
11 × 52 =	9 × 18 =	38 × 9 =	11 × 9 =

PART II MULTIPLICATION

9) Can multiply any number by 100 mentally

For example, 100 × 17, 42 × 100, 100 × 160, 0·5 × 100, 100 × 0·04

ACTIVITY 9.1

Resources
- none

T	U
	7
7	0

×10

Moving digits again

This activity extends the work on multiplying by 10 in Activity 7.1, *'Moving digits'* on page 17. Draw tens and units columns on the board, as shown on the left.

Ask children for a single-digit number, for example, 7. Write it in the units column. Ask children for the answer when this is multiplied by 10. Write down this answer. Continue this process, noting down all the numbers beneath each other in the correct columns as shown.

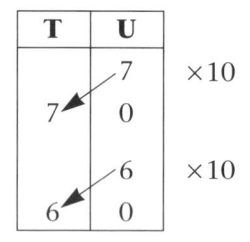

T	U	
	7	×10
7	0	
	6	×10
6	0	

Draw children's attention to what is happening to the digits when we multiply by 10, i.e. they move one place to the left and a 0 fills the space left behind. This helps to avoid the 'add a nought' which causes difficulties when decimals are encountered. Now introduce multiplying by 100 in the same way.

Th	H	T	U	
			4	×100
	4	0	0	
			5	×100
	5	0	0	
		1	2	×100
1	2	0	0	

Emphasise the movement of the digits *two* places to the left and the arrival of *two* zeros which simply fill the columns left behind.

ACTIVITY 9.2

Resources
- 'Making a move!' sheet on page 25
- calculator

Making a move

This activity begins by revisiting multiplying by 10 before moving on to multiplying whole numbers and decimal numbers by 100. Column headings are initially emphasised and should be used by children in their written recording. A calculator can be used for checking.

ACTIVITY 9.3

Resources
- 'Snowballing' sheet on page 26
- calculator

Snowballing

This activity begins by revisiting multiplying by 10 before multiplying whole numbers by 100. Children should set out column headings in their books to help them to move the digits. A calculator can be used for checking.

9 CAN MULTIPLY ANY NUMBER BY 100 MENTALLY

9.2

Name

Making a move

Use a calculator to see what happens when you multiply these numbers by 10. Write the answer underneath each one.
What do you notice? See if you can work out any without using a calculator.
As each digit becomes ten times bigger it appears to move! For example,
2 units becomes 10 × 2 units = 20 units = 2 tens
and the '2' moves over into the tens column and so on.

× 10

Th	H	T	U · t
		5	4
	1	5	9
	6	0	7 · 1

Now try multiplying these numbers by 100. How many places do the digits move and in which direction?

....
....
....

× 100

TTh	Th	H	T	U · t
			6	5
			4	0 ·
		9	3	2 · 3
		3	3	0 · 8
		7	0	7 · 0

Fill in the missing numbers in the tables below.

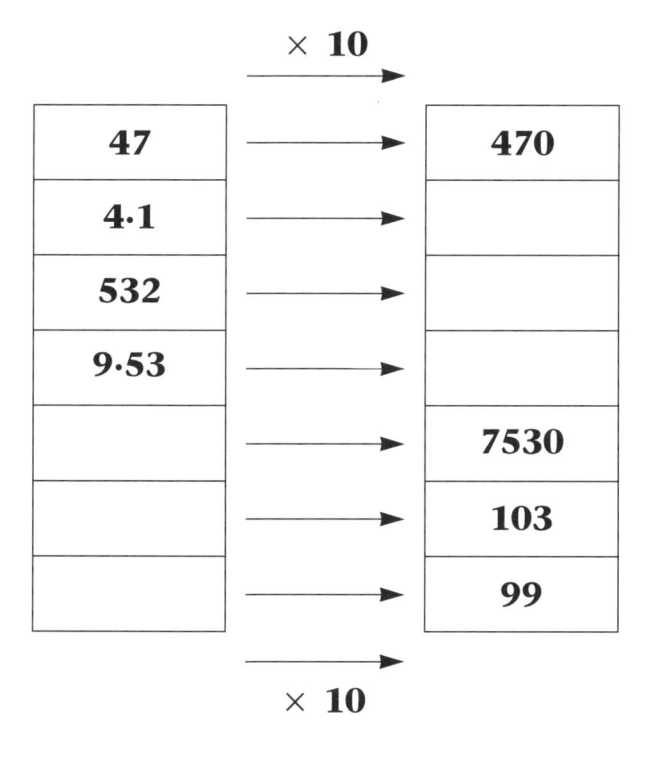

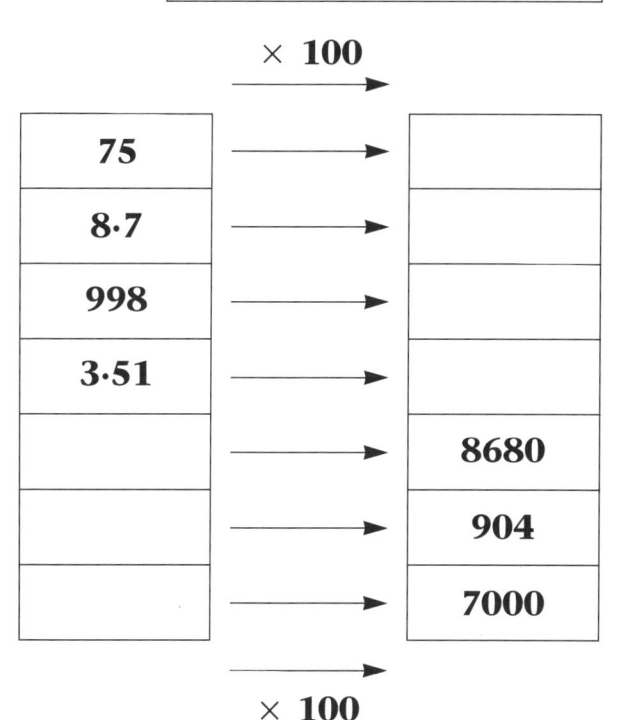

× 10 →

47	→	470
4·1	→	
532	→	
9·53	→	
	→	7530
	→	103
	→	99

× 10 →

× 100 →

75	→	
8·7	→	
998	→	
3·51	→	
	→	8680
	→	904
	→	7000

× 100 →

KS2 Numeracy Pack © Letts Educational, 1999   25

PART II   MULTIPLICATION

Name ....

Snowballing

9.3

As these snowballs roll down the hill they get larger. Follow the instructions to make the numbers inside them bigger. Write column headings in your book and write the missing numbers in the columns as you go down the hills.

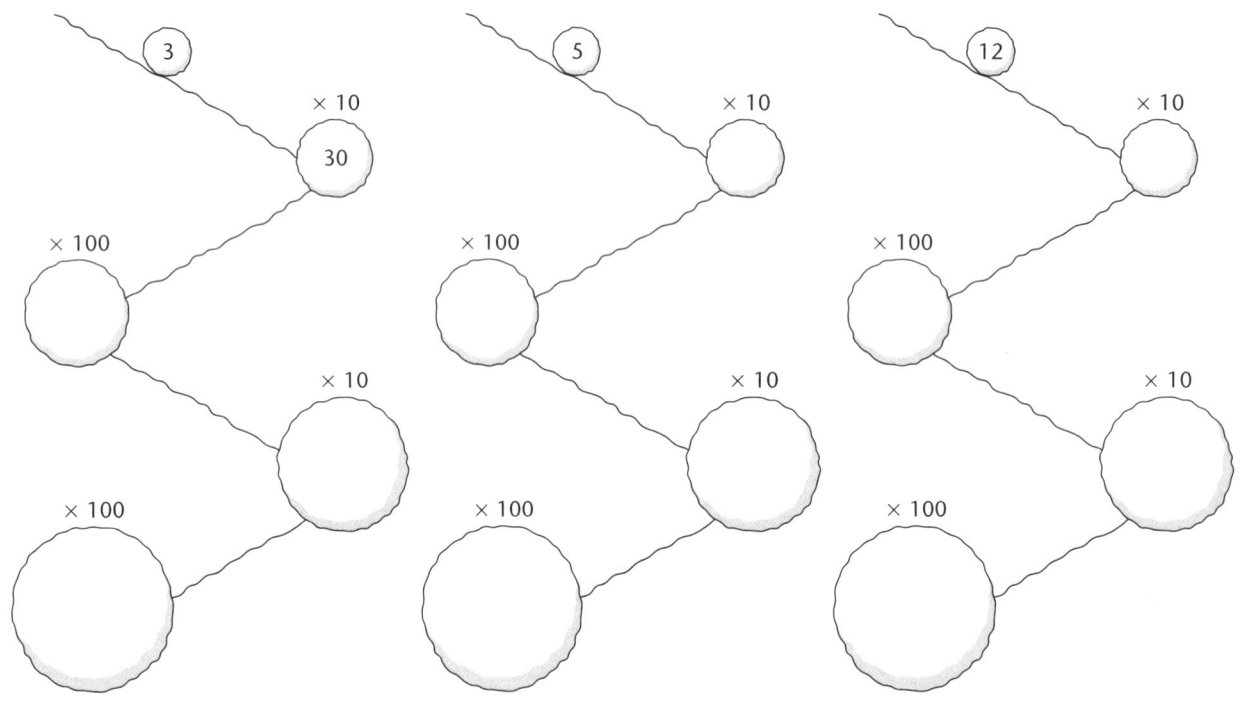

Hill 1: 3 → × 10 → 30 → × 100 → ○ → × 10 → ○ → × 100 → ○

Hill 2: 5 → × 10 → ○ → × 100 → ○ → × 10 → ○ → × 100 → ○

Hill 3: 12 → × 10 → ○ → × 100 → ○ → × 10 → ○ → × 100 → ○

Now try these – the hillside is very steep and the snowballs are growing very quickly!

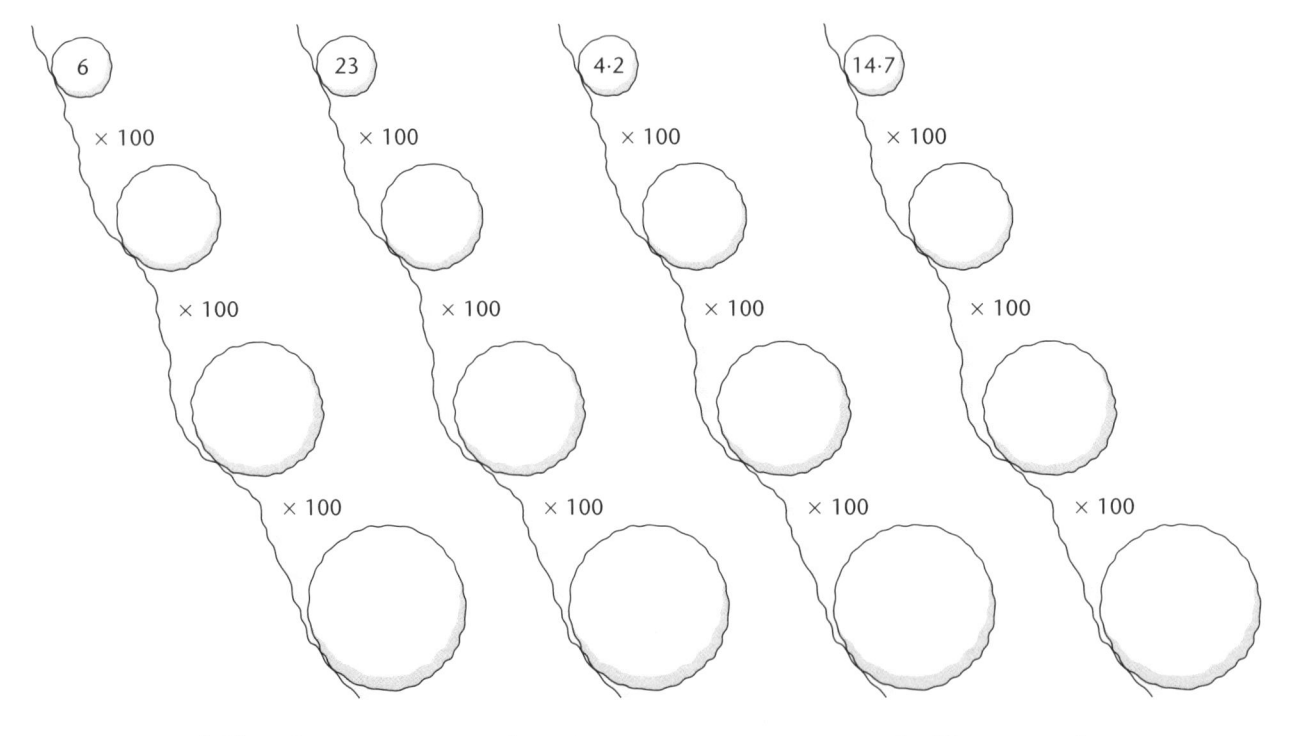

Hill A: 6 → × 100 → ○ → × 100 → ○ → × 100 → ○

Hill B: 23 → × 100 → ○ → × 100 → ○ → × 100 → ○

Hill C: 4·2 → × 100 → ○ → × 100 → ○ → × 100 → ○

Hill D: 14·7 → × 100 → ○ → × 100 → ○ → × 100 → ○

Draw some hills of your own and make up your own snowballing numbers.

26   KS2 Numeracy Pack © Letts Educational, 1999

10 Can multiply any number by 99 or 101, etc., mentally

For example, 4 × 99, 25 × 99, 98 × 25, 36 × 101, 101 × 122

Activity 10.1

Resources
- none

A hundred and one

Once children are comfortable with multiplying by 100, they can use this skill as the basis for multiplying by 99 and 101. Ask children to multiply by 100, for example, 15 × 100, 23 × 100, etc. Now develop these, as below.

| 15 × 100 = 1500 | so | 15 × 101 = 15 × 100 + 15 × 1 |
| 23 × 100 = 2300 | so | 23 × 101 = 23 × 100 + 23 × 1 |

This can be shortened to   23 × 101 = 23 × 100 + 23   as soon as the children understand what is happening.

Ask them to solve further calculations in the same way, emphasising the strategy involved.

Activity 10.2

Resources
- none

Ninety-nines

Activity 10.1, 'A hundred and one' can naturally be used to develop competence in multiplying by ninety-nine. Once again reiterate multiplying by 100 and then subtract one lot of the number being multiplied.

| 15 × 100 = 1500 | so | 15 × 99 = 15 × 100 − 15 × 1 |
| 23 × 100 = 2300 | so | 23 × 99 = 23 × 100 − 23 × 1 |

As above, this can quickly become   23 × 99 = 23 × 100 − 23.

Activity 10.3

Resources
- none

Target times

On the board, draw two rings around a circle as shown. Write ×99 or ×101 in the centre circle. In the first ring write a range of numbers to multiply. Ask children to come up and multiply these numbers by the centre number and to write these in the outer layer.

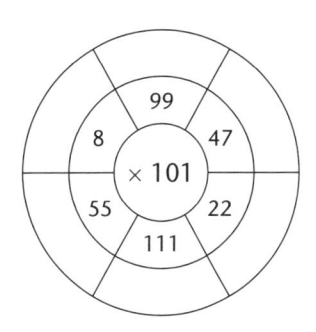

Activity 10.4

Resources
- 'Cook's maths' sheet on page 28

Cook's maths

This sheet provides an opportunity for children to practise and consolidate multiplying by 101 and 99 in the context of money. Later questions extend this by asking children to find multiples of 101 and 99 by doubling.

PART II MULTIPLICATION

10.4

Name ....

Cook's maths

The school cook is at the supermarket. There are 101 children who have school dinners (and sometimes 2 are away!). Help her to work out how much she will spend.

1 1 fish finger costs 5p. What is the cost of:

101 fish fingers? .... 99 fish fingers? ....

2 1 apple costs 17p. What is the cost of:

101 apples? .... 99 apples? ....

3 10 cans of cola cost £4.20. What is the cost of:

101 cans? .... 99 cans? ....

4 10 packets of crisps cost £3.70. How much are:

101 packets? .... 99 packets? ....

5 1 sausage costs 20p. How much are:

101 sausages? .... 99 sausages? ....

202 sausages? .... 198 sausages? ....

11 Can multiply any number by 1000 mentally

For example, 42 × 1000, 1000 × 127, 0·4 × 1000, 1·02 × 1000

ACTIVITY 11.1

Resources
- none

Moving digits again

This activity extends the work on multiplying by 10 and 100 in units 7 and 9. Draw the following on the board.

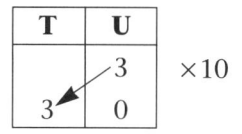

T	U
	3	×10
3	0

Draw children's attention to what is happening to the digits when we multiply by 10 and 100, i.e. they move to the left and zeros fill the empty columns left behind. This helps to avoid the 'add a nought' which causes difficulties when decimals are encountered. Now introduce multiplying by 100 in the same way.

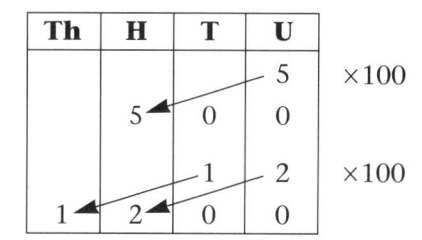

Th	H	T	U
			5	×100
	5	0	0
		1	2	×100
1	2	0	0

Emphasise the movement of the digits two places to the left and the arrival of two zeros which simply fill the columns left behind. Multiplying by 1000 can be developed simply as an extension to this.

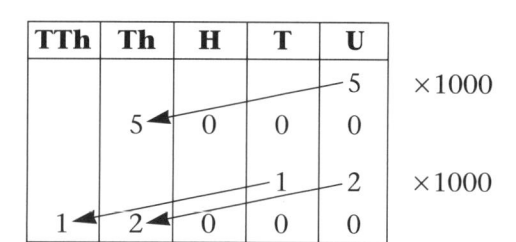

TTh	Th	H	T	U
				5	×1000
	5	0	0	0
			1	2	×1000
1	2	0	0	0

Activity 11.2, 'Hurdles race' can be used to exemplify these movements for a single digit and to emphasise the inverse natures of multiplication and division.

PART II MULTIPLICATION

ACTIVITY 11.2

Resources
- resource sheet 3 on page 60

Hurdles race

On the board draw four horizontal rows to represent race tracks, as shown. Mark on vertical dotted lines to represent 'hurdles'

M	HTh	TTh	Th	H	T	U
						7
						9
						3
						8

Split the class into four groups and explain that each group is taking part in a race. The aim is to move a single digit across from the right-hand column to the left-hand column. Write the column headings above each column as shown. Each group can choose a digit for their team. Write these digits in the units column, one in each row. A child from each group takes it in turns to choose one of the six cards marked ×10, ×100, ×1000, ÷10, ÷100, and ÷1000 on resource sheet 3 on page 60. (A team cannot begin until they have selected a multiplication card.) Their digit then moves the number of columns across and zeros are written in the columns they have left. From this point on, if a move is possible (either multiplication or division) their digit moves. The winning team is the one with the digit that reaches the millions column first.

The game can be played beginning with 2-digit numbers, and tenths and hundredths columns can be introduced to demonstrate division producing decimal answers.

ACTIVITY 11.3

Resources
- 'Moving!' sheet on page 31

Moving!

This activity begins by revisiting multiplying by 10 and 100 before multiplying whole numbers by 1000. Column headings are initially emphasised and should be used by children in their written recording.

ACTIVITY 11.4

Resources
- 'Moving with decimals' sheet on page 32
- calculator

Moving with decimals

This activity begins by revisiting multiplying by 10 and 100 before moving on to multiplying whole numbers and decimal numbers by 1000. Column headings are initially emphasised and should be used by children in their written recording. A calculator can be used for checking.

11 CAN MULTIPLY ANY NUMBER BY 1000 MENTALLY
11.3

Name ....

Moving!

Use a calculator to see what happens when you multiply these numbers by 10. Write the answer underneath each one.
What do you notice? See if you can work out any without using a calculator.

× **10**

Th	H	T	U
		6	5
	4	0	7

Now try multiplying these numbers by 100. How many places do the digits move and in which direction?

....

....

× **100**

TTh	Th	H	T	U
			3	8
		2	6	1
		7	1	0

Now try multiplying these numbers by 1000. How many places do the digits move and in which direction?

....

....

× **1000**

HTh	TTh	Th	H	T	U
					2
				4	6
			3	2	8
			5	0	2
			3	0	0

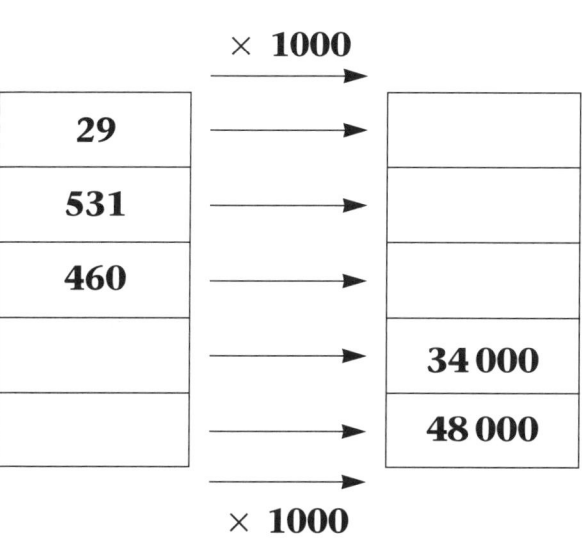

Fill in the missing numbers in the tables below.

× **100**

29	→	2900
103	→	
5234	→	
	→	7300
	→	65 000

× **100**

× **1000**

29	→	
531	→	
460	→	
	→	34 000
	→	48 000

× **1000**

PART II   MULTIPLICATION

(11.4)

Name ....

Moving with decimals

Use a calculator to see what happens when you multiply these numbers by 10. Write the answer underneath each one.
What do you notice? See if you can work out any without using a calculator.

× 10

Th	H	T	U · t
		3	5
	5	1	7 · 2

Now try multiplying these numbers by 100. How many places do the digits move and in which direction?

....

....

× 100

TTh	Th	H	T	U · t
			9	8
			6	0 · 7
		6	6	9 · 3

Now try multiplying these numbers by 1000. How many places do the digits move and in which direction?

....

....

....

× 1000

HTh	TTh	Th	H	T	U · t
					2
				4 · 6
			3	2	8 · 4
		5	0	2 · 7
		3	0	0 · 0

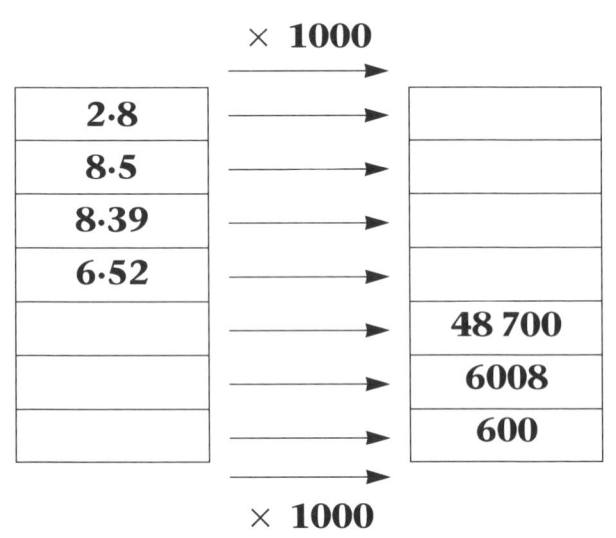

Fill in the missing numbers in the tables below.

× 100

2·8	→	280
2·9	→	
8·39	→	
6·521	→	
	→	6520
	→	603
	→	68

× 100

× 1000

2·8	→	
8·5	→	
8·39	→	
6·52	→	
	→	48 700
	→	6008
	→	600

× 1000

32   KS2 Numeracy Pack © Letts Educational, 1999

12 Can multiply any number by 999 or 1001, etc. mentally

For example, 5 × 999, 999 × 9, 7 × 1001, 1001 × 150, 0·3 × 1002

Activity 12.1

Resources
- none

A thousand and one

Once children are comfortable with multiplying by 1000, they can use this skill as the basis for multiplying by 999 and 1001. Ask children to multiply by 1000, for example, 17 × 1000, 25 × 1000, etc. Now develop these, as shown.

| 17 × 1000 = 17 000 | so | 17 × 1001 = 17 × 1000 + 17 × 1 |
| 25 × 1000 = 25 000 | so | 25 × 1001 = 25 × 1000 + 25 × 1 |

This can be shortened to   25 × 1001 = 25 × 1000 + 25   as soon as the children understand what is happening.

Ask them to solve further calculations in the same way, emphasising the strategy involved. A good understanding of place value is required. For more difficult calculations some children may need to make mental jottings as they go along. For example,

$$1001 \times 891 = 891\,000$$
$$+ \quad 891$$

This method, however, is still much easier than attempting 3/4-digit by 3-digit long multiplication. Mental jottings assist children to 'hold numbers in their heads'.

Activity 12.2

Resources
- none

Nine hundred and ninety-nines

Activity 12.1, 'A thousand and one' can naturally be used to develop competence in multiplying by nine hundred and ninety-nine. Once again reiterate multiplying by 1000 and then subtract one lot of the number being multiplied.

| 17 × 1000 = 17 000 | so | 17 × 999 = 17 × 1000 – 17 × 1 |
| 25 × 1000 = 25 000 | so | 25 × 999 = 25 × 1000 – 25 × 1 |

As above, this can quickly become   25 × 999 = 25 × 1000 – 25.

A good understanding of place value is required for multiplication of this kind. For more difficult calculations some children may need to make mental jottings as they go along.

For example,

$$999 \times 891 = 891\,000$$
$$- \quad 891$$

This method, however, is still much easier than attempting 3-digit by 3-digit long multiplication. Mental jottings assist children to 'hold numbers in their heads'.

PART II   MULTIPLICATION

ACTIVITY 12.3

Resources
- none

999, Fire, police or ambulance?

On the board draw the following diagram, placing ×999 in the centre door.

[Illustration of a burning block of flats with windows showing the numbers: 13, 100, 77, 8, 90, 22, 14, 40, 3, 54, and a central door labelled ×999]

Explain that this block of flats is on fire and to put out the flames they must multiply each number by 999 correctly. It is important to calculate answers quickly to prevent any casualties. Give a time limit in which they have to solve each question which is appropriate to the children concerned, for example, 15 seconds. Children can be asked to come up in turn and write an answer on the board, or can solve these individually or in groups, recording their answers on paper.

The activity can be repeated using ×1001 or any other number or operation.

ACTIVITY 12.4

Resources
- 'At the match' sheet on page 35

At the match

This sheet provides an opportunity for children to practise and consolidate multiplying by 1001 and 999, etc. in the context of sales of food and drink at a football match.

12 CAN MULTIPLY ANY NUMBER BY 999 OR 1001, ETC. MENTALLY

12.4

Name ....

At the match

Stalybridge Celtic are a non-league football team. Yesterday they were playing at home and a crowd of about 1000 was there. Most people had things to eat and drink during the match. Work out how much was spent on each item.

(1) Teas

1 cup of tea costs 40p. What is the cost of:

1001 cups of tea? .... 999 cups? ....

(2) Meat pies

1 meat pie costs 85p. What is the cost of:

1001 pies? .... 999 pies? ....

(3) Colas

10 cans of cola cost £4.20. What is the cost of:

1001 cans? .... 999 cans? ....

(4) Crisps

10 packets of crisps cost £3.70. How much are:

1001 packets? .... 999 packets? ....

(5) Hot dogs

1 hot dog costs 20p. How much are:

1001 hot dogs? .... 999 hot dogs? ....

2002 hot dogs? .... 1998 hot dogs? ....

KS2 Numeracy Pack © Letts Educational, 1999   35

PART II   MULTIPLICATION

⑬ Can multiply two multiples of 10, 100, 1000 mentally

For example, 20 × 40, 30 × 90, 400 × 20, 500 × 500, 20 × 5000

ACTIVITY 13.1

Resources
- none

Roots

On the board write a series of questions like the ones here.

6 × 4	=	6 × 40	=	6 × 400	=	6 × 4000	=
60 × 4	=	600 × 4	=	6000 × 4	=	60 × 40	=
600 × 40 =		6000 × 40 =		600 × 400 =		6000 × 400 = etc.

Ask the children to answer any of the questions that they can. Discuss the strategies they used. These may include multiplying 6 × 4 and then attaching the required number of zeros. Write the answers on the board as you go, linking any questions that give the same answer, for example, 6 × 400 and 60 × 40.

The activity can be repeated using another tables fact as the root of subsequent questions. Activity 13.3, 'How many zeros?' can be used for consolidation and practice of this idea.

ACTIVITY 13.2

Resources
- 'More circuits! cards' on page 37

More circuits!

Use the cards on page 37 for this activity. Give one card to each child and read the question on one card aloud, for example, '50 × 20 is...?'. One child in the group will have a card which has the answer to the question, which they call out, followed by the question on their card. Play continues until the answer on the original card is reached.

ACTIVITY 13.3

Resources
- 'How many zeros?' sheet on page 38

How many zeros?

This activity provides practice in multiplying two multiples of 10, 100 or 1000 by encouraging children to build up a series of calculations which emphasise the patterns involved, for example, 5 × 30, 5 × 300, 5 × 3000, etc.

More circuits! cards

13 CAN MULTIPLY TWO MULTIPLES OF 10, 100, 1000 MENTALLY

13.2

400	**300**	**1000**	**1200**
30 × 10 =	50 × 20 =	40 × 30 =	500 × 20 =

10 000	**5400**	**5600**	**12 000**
60 × 90 =	80 × 70 =	300 × 40 =	500 × 500 =

250 000	**1800**	**9000**	**2500**
60 × 30 =	90 × 100 =	50 × 50 =	130 × 40 =

5200	**1600**	**7200**	**150 000**
160 × 10 =	80 × 90 =	5000 × 30 =	40 × 10 =

KS2 Numeracy Pack © Letts Educational, 1999

PART II MULTIPLICATION

13.3

Name ....

How many zeros?

Work these questions out in your head and write down the answers. Draw a line to join any questions that give the same answer. One has been done for you.

$5 \times 3 =$

(1) $5 \times 30 = 150$ (2) $5 \times 300 =$ (3) $5 \times 3000 =$

(4) $50 \times 3 = 150$ (5) $500 \times 3 =$ (6) $5000 \times 3 =$

(7) $50 \times 30 =$ (8) $500 \times 30 =$ (9) $500 \times 300 =$

$7 \times 4 =$

(10) $7 \times 40 =$ (11) $7 \times 400 =$ (12) $7 \times 4000 =$

(13) $70 \times 4 =$ (14) $700 \times 4 =$ (15) $7000 \times 4 =$

(16) $70 \times 40 =$ (17) $700 \times 40 =$ (18) $700 \times 400 =$

$6 \times 9 =$

(19) $6 \times 90 =$ (20) $6 \times 900 =$ (21) $6 \times 9000 =$

(22) $60 \times 9 =$ (23) $600 \times 9 =$ (24) $6000 \times 9 =$

(25) $60 \times 90 =$ (26) $600 \times 90 =$ (27) $600 \times 900 =$

(28) $6000 \times 90 =$ (29) $6000 \times 900 =$ (30) $6000 \times 9000 =$

48 000

(31) Find as many questions as you can with an answer of 48 000.

14 Can multiply a near multiple of 10, 100, 1000 by a multiple of 10, 100, 1000 mentally

For example, 21 × 40, 30 × 91, 60 × 71, 19 × 400, 500 × 498

Activity 14.1

Resources
- none

Spreading roots

This activity follows on from Activity 13.1, 'Roots' on page 36. Once children are comfortable with multiplying two multiples of ten, for example, 60 × 40, we can help them to use this skill as a basis for calculations such as 61 × 40 and 400 × 39.

On the board write a series of questions like the ones below to remind children of the strategies for multiplying multiples of ten, as in 60 × 40. This may consist of multiplying 6 × 4 and then attaching two zeros.

6 × 40 =   60 × 40 =   60 × 400 =   600 × 400 =

Now remind them of the strategy for multiplying by 9, 99, 11 and 101, that is, to first multiply by 10 or 100 and then to add or subtract one lot of the number, as here.

15 × 100 = 1500   so   15 × 101 = 15 × 100 + 15
15 × 100 = 1500   so   15 × 99 = 15 × 100 − 15

On the board write questions like these:

50 × 40 =   51 × 40 =   49 × 40 =
90 × 30 =   91 × 30 =   89 × 30 =

and help the children to see that the strategies they already possess will help them to solve these.

Activity 14.2, 'The maze' can be used as consolidation of this idea.

Activity 14.2

Resources
- 'The maze' sheet on page 40
- two counters
- calculator

The maze

This is a game for two players. It provides an opportunity for practising multiplying a near multiple of 10, 100, 1000 by a multiple of 10, 100, 1000, for example, 21 × 40, 300 × 91. The object of the game is to cross the maze to reach your opponent's (Home) by answering the questions. Players can choose different routes through the maze. The player who is first to reach the opponent's (Home) wins. Wrong answers give the opponent an extra go. A calculator can be used to settle any disputes.

PART II   MULTIPLICATION

The maze

Player 1 begins with a counter on **Home 1**. Player 2 begins with a counter on **Home 2**. Take it in turns to move to the next question in the maze and to work out the answer. You can choose any route through the maze that you like. If you get an answer wrong the other player gets 2 goes. The winner is the player who is first to get their counter to the other player's **Home**.

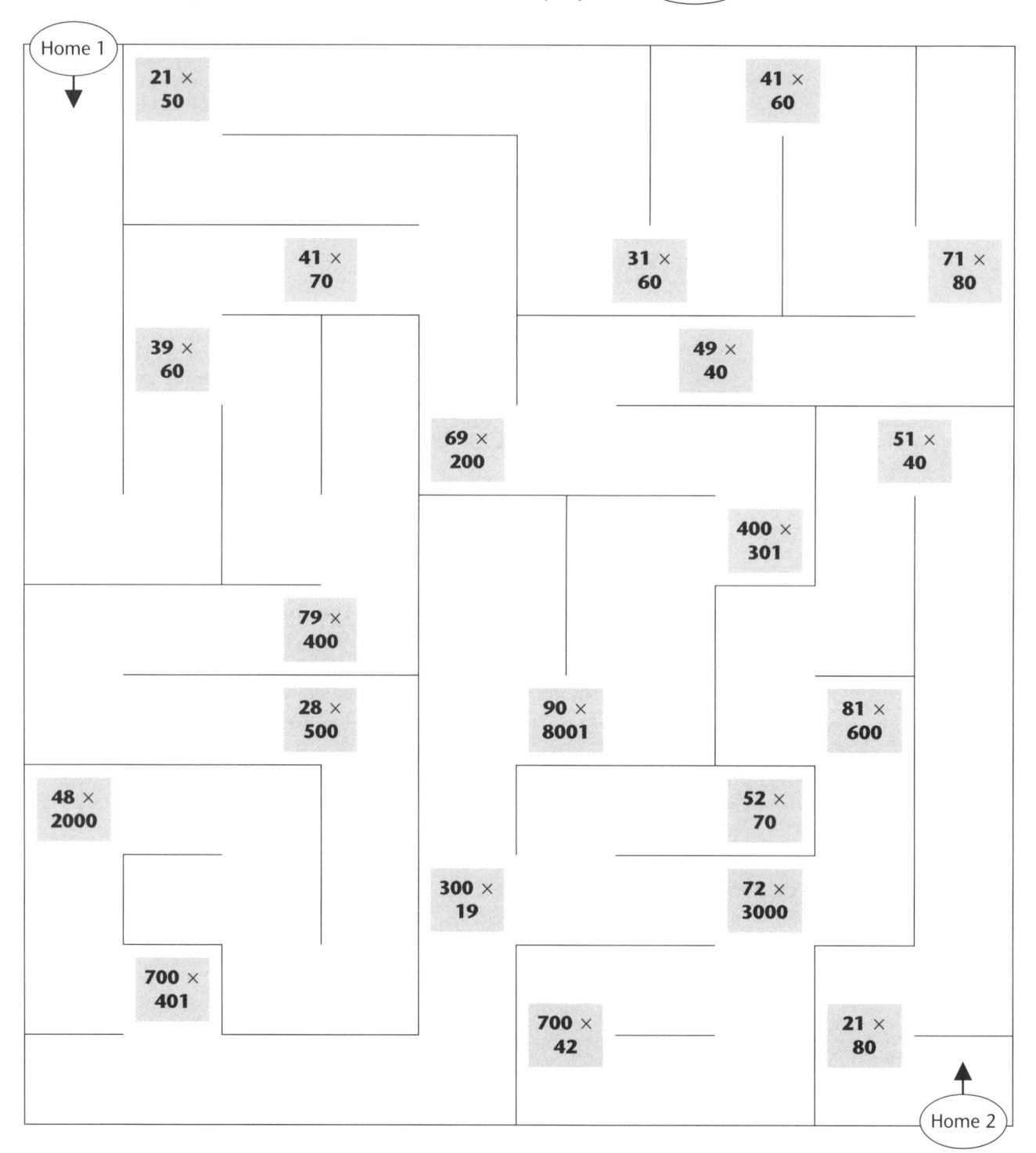

Home 1

- 21 × 50
- 41 × 60
- 41 × 70
- 31 × 60
- 71 × 80
- 39 × 60
- 49 × 40
- 69 × 200
- 51 × 40
- 400 × 301
- 79 × 400
- 28 × 500
- 90 × 8001
- 81 × 600
- 48 × 2000
- 52 × 70
- 300 × 19
- 72 × 3000
- 700 × 401
- 700 × 42
- 21 × 80

Home 2

40   KS2 Numeracy Pack © Letts Educational, 1999

15 Can multiply any 2-digit number by a multiple of 10, 100, 1000 mentally

For example, 14 × 20, 13 × 50, 600 × 52, 63 × 500, 22 × 4000

Activity 15.1

Resources
- none

Finding roots

This activity builds on the work in Activity 13.1, '*Roots*' on page 36 and Activity 14.1, '*Spreading roots*' on page 39. Once children are comfortable with multiplying near multiples of ten by multiples of ten, for example, 41 × 600, we can help them to use this skill as a basis for multiplying any 2-digit number by a multiple of 10.

On the board write a series of questions like the ones below to remind children of the strategies for multiplying by near multiples of ten, as in 41 × 60 and 41 × 600. This may consist of first multiplying 4 × 6 and then attaching two zeros to give the answer to 40 × 60 and three zeros to give the answer to 40 × 600 before adding one lot of 60 or 600.

$$4 \times 6 = 24 \quad 40 \times 60 = 2400 \quad 41 \times 60 = 2460$$
$$4 \times 6 = 24 \quad 40 \times 600 = 24\,000 \quad 41 \times 600 = 24\,600$$

On the board write questions like these.

$$23 \times 60 = \quad 36 \times 40 = \quad 65 \times 30 =$$

Discuss how we might solve these and help children to develop a suitable strategy. For example, for 23 × 60 we might develop our strategy to multiply 20 × 60 as follows.

$$23 \times 60 = 20 \times 60 + 3 \times 60 = 1200 + 180 = 1380$$

Activity 15.2, '*The maze revisited*' can be used for consolidation of this idea.

Activity 15.2

Resources
- 'The maze revisited' sheet on page 42
- calculator
- two counters

The maze revisited

This is a game for two players based on Activity 14.2, '*The maze*' on page 39 for familiarity.

It provides opportunities for practising multiplying a multiple of 10 by any 2-digit number, for example, 27 × 40, 300 × 94. The object of the game is to cross the maze to reach your opponent's (Home) by answering the questions. Players can choose different routes through the maze. The player who is first to reach the opponent's (Home) wins. Wrong answers give the opponent an extra go. A calculator can be used to settle any disputes.

Activity 15.3

Resources
- 'Extra circuits! cards' on page 43

Extra circuits!

Give one card to each child and read the question on one card aloud, for example, '72 × 100 = …?'. One child in the group will have a card which has the answer to the question, which they call out, followed by the question on their card. Play continues until the answer on the original card is reached.

PART II   MULTIPLICATION

The maze revisited

15.2

Player 1 begins with a counter on **Home 1**. Player 2 begins with a counter on **Home 2**. Take it in turns to move to the next question in the maze and to work out the answer. You can choose any route through the maze that you like. If you get the answer wrong the other player gets 2 goes. The winner is the player who is first to get their counter to the other player's **Home**.

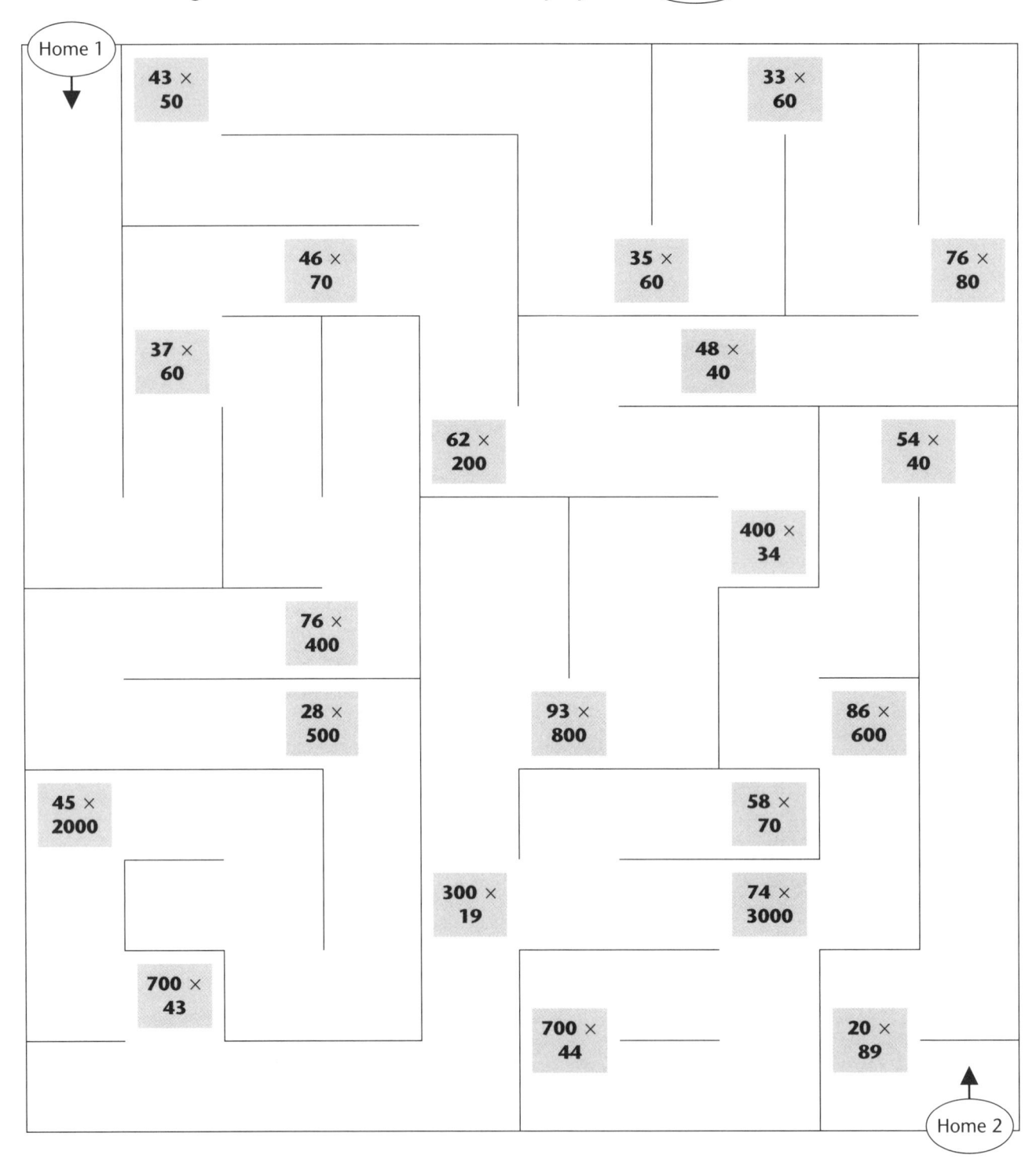

Home 1

43 × 50			33 × 60	
46 × 70		35 × 60		76 × 80
37 × 60		48 × 40		
	62 × 200			54 × 40
			400 × 34	
76 × 400				
28 × 500		93 × 800		86 × 600
45 × 2000			58 × 70	
		300 × 19	74 × 3000	
700 × 43		700 × 44		20 × 89

Home 2

42   KS2 Numeracy Pack © Letts Educational, 1999

Extra circuits! cards

420	1500	1350	31 500
30 × 50 =	45 × 30 =	500 × 63 =	40 × 15 =
600	**2850**	**7200**	**17 200**
30 × 95 =	72 × 100 =	86 × 200 =	35 × 300 =
10 500	**1080**	**3000**	**21 000**
27 × 40 =	50 × 60 =	500 × 42 =	80 × 83 =
6640	**31 200**	**6750**	**88 000**
600 × 52 =	90 × 75 =	22 × 4000 =	42 × 10 =

PART II   MULTIPLICATION

⑯ Can multiply a decimal (1 decimal place) by a single digit mentally

For example, 5 × 0·5, 6 × 1·2, 7 × 1·5, 8·2 × 5

ACTIVITY 16.1

Resources
- none

Multiplying decimals

The ability to approximate an answer is a useful tool when multiplying decimal numbers. Write the following question on the board.

6 × 3·2

Ask 'About how many whole ones will be in the answer?'. Encourage children to multiply the 6 by the 3 to provide a rough idea of the answer. So we know the answer will be 'about 18' or 'a bit more than 18', etc. Now multiply 6 × 32.

6 × 32 = 192

Given our knowledge that the answer will be 'about 18' we can see that the answer to 6 × 3·2 is 19·2.

6 × 3·2 = 19·2

Discuss what the other possibilities are, for example, 192, 1·92, to emphasise that 19·2 is the answer.

ACTIVITY 16.2

Resources
- 'Dizzy decimals' sheet on page 45
- counters

Dizzy decimals

This is an activity for practice in multiplying decimals. Children pick two numbers from the 'tray' and multiply them. If the answer appears in the grid they cover it with a counter of their colour (alternatively it can be coloured in). The winner is the first player to get three counters in a line in any direction.

ACTIVITY 16.3

Resources
- none

Decimal investigation

Children can work in groups to do this investigation. Draw a box on the board and write in some decimals (to 1 decimal place) and whole numbers beneath 10, like this.

3·6	5	1·8
6·2	4·2	8·4
7·5	9	3·2

Explain to the children that they will be trying to make these numbers, using the following method.

Choose any of the digits, **0 1 2 3 4 5 6 7 8 9.**

Select three and arrange them like this.

☐ · ☐ × ☐ =

For example, 1·6 × 2 = 3·2.

Note that the box on the right, the multiplier, cannot be 1.

How many different numbers under 10 can they generate? Children can work in groups to do this investigation.

44

Dizzy decimals

Take turns to choose a number from each box.
Multiply them together and see if the answer is on the grid.
If the answer is in the grid, put a counter on it.
The first person to get 3 counters in a line wins.

Box 1

6·2	5·8	3·7
3·2	4·5	5·6

Box 2

2	3	4	5
6	7	8	9

31	11·6	11·1	40·6	49·6	18
4·6	22·4	18·6	17·4	13·5	28
7·4	14·8	6·9	16·1	33·3	46·4
20·7	52·2	29	40·8	61·2	25·9
40·5	12·4	13·8	22·2	23·2	39·2

Design your own game like this one using your own numbers in the boxes and the grid.

PART III   DIVISION

⑰ Can divide a 2-digit number by a single digit without or with remainders mentally

For example, 18 ÷ 2, 28 ÷ 4, 47 ÷ 9, 49 ÷ 6, 29 ÷ 3

ACTIVITY 17.1

Resources
- 'Head it!' sheet on page 47
- calculator is optional

Head it!

This sheet provides children with opportunities to divide a 2-digit by a 1-digit number.

The activity also requires children to create division questions of their own which produce particular answers. A calculator can be used to check these.

ACTIVITY 17.2

Resources
- three dice
- calculator

Mental approximation

This is a game for two, three or four players. Each player, in turn, rolls two dice in a line. The dice on the left gives the tens digit and the dice on the right gives the units digit so the top two dice on the right show 54.

The third dice is rolled to give a 1-digit number, in this case 4. Each player estimates how many times 4 goes into 54. For example, player 1 might estimate 15 times, player 2, 12 times. When all the players have written their estimate they use a calculator to see who was closest. The player who gave the closest estimate gets a point and play continues. The game can be extended by re-numbering the dice from 5 to 10 or by using decahedron dice numbered 1–10.

ACTIVITY 17.3

Resources
- 'Short circuits! cards' on page 48

Short circuits!

Use the cards on page 48 for this activity. Give one card to each child and read the question on one card aloud, for example, 'Thirty-two divided by four is...?'. One child in the group will have a card which has the answer to the question, which they call out, followed by the question on their card. Play continues until the answer on the original card is reached.

17 CAN DIVIDE A 2-DIGIT NUMBER BY A SINGLE DIGIT WITHOUT OR WITH REMAINDERS MENTALLY

17.1

Name

Head it!

Answer these questions in your head and write down your answers.

1) 77 ÷ 7 = ... **2)** 85 ÷ 5 = ... **3)** 96 ÷ 6 = ...

4) 84 ÷ 7 = ... **5)** 54 ÷ 3 = ... **6)** 66 ÷ 6 = ...

7) 96 ÷ 8 = ... **8)** 88 ÷ 8 = ... **9)** 52 ÷ 4 = ...

10) 74 ÷ 2 = ... **11)** 90 ÷ 6 = ... **12)** 98 ÷ 7 = ...

13) 84 ÷ 5 = ... **14)** 92 ÷ 3 = ... **15)** 92 ÷ 6 = ...

Here are the answers to some division questions.
Write some questions that give these answers.

16) .... ÷ .... = 12 **17)** .... ÷ .... = 16 **18)** .... ÷ .... = 8

19) .... ÷ .... = 13 **20)** .... ÷ .... = 22 **21)** .... ÷ .... = 19

22) .... ÷ .... = 14 **23)** .... ÷ .... = 17 **24)** .... ÷ .... = 34

Write as many division questions as you can think of which give the answer...

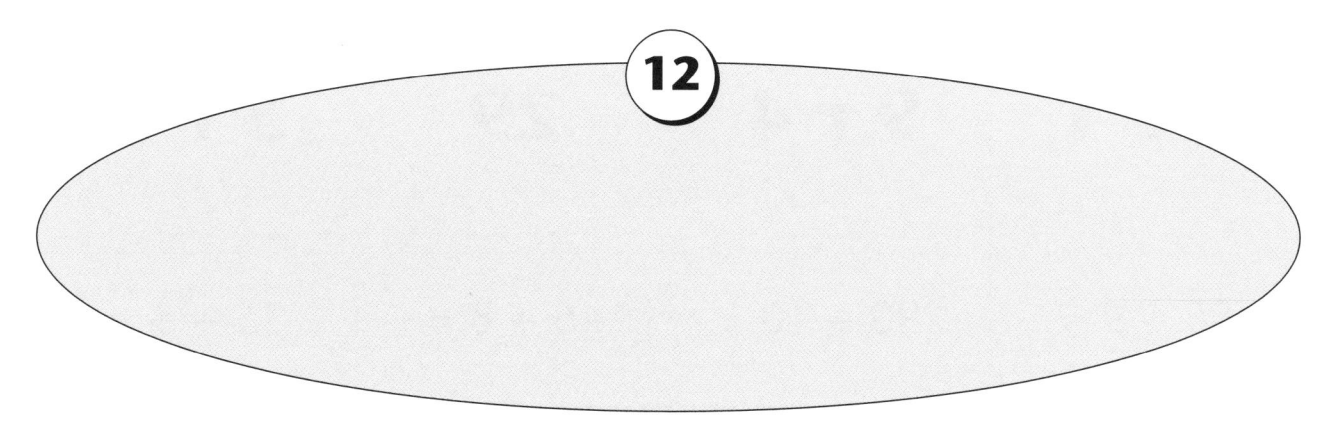

12

KS2 Numeracy Pack © Letts Educational, 1999

PART III DIVISION

17.3

Short circuits! cards

7	**9 r 2**	**17**	**10 r 6**
29 ÷ 3 =	51 ÷ 3 =	86 ÷ 8 =	59 ÷ 9 =
6 r 5	**8**	**4 r 1**	**13**
32 ÷ 4 =	21 ÷ 5 =	91 ÷ 7 =	65 ÷ 9 =
7 r 2	**6 r 1**	**15 r 1**	**19**
49 ÷ 8 =	31 ÷ 2 =	19 ÷ 1 =	43 ÷ 6 =
7 r 1	**9 r 4**	**29**	**5 r 6**
85 ÷ 9 =	290 ÷ 10 =	46 ÷ 8 =	35 ÷ 5 =

18 Can divide a multiple of 10 by 10, and a multiple of 100 by 10 or 100 mentally

For example, 160 ÷ 10, 270 ÷ 10, 900 ÷ 100, 7800 ÷ 100

ACTIVITY 18.1

Resources
- none

Moving right

This activity demonstrates the effect of dividing by 10 and 100. Draw tens and units columns on the board.

Write a 2-digit multiple of 10 in the columns, for example, 70. Ask children for the answer when this is divided by 10. Write down this answer. Continue this process, noting down all the numbers beneath each other in the correct columns. For example,

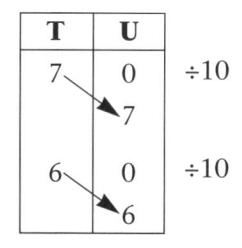

T	U	
7	0	÷10
	7	
6	0	÷10
	6	

Draw children's attention to what is happening to the digits when we divide by 10, i.e. they move one place to the right and, as a result, any multiple of 10 will lose a zero. Now introduce dividing by 100 in the same way.

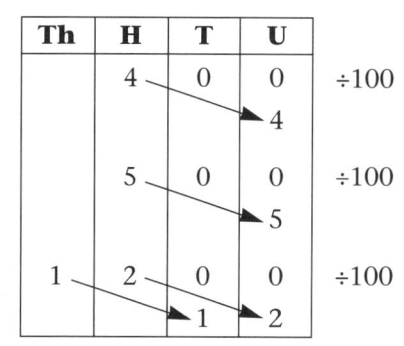

Th	H	T	U	
	4	0	0	÷100
			4	
	5	0	0	÷100
			5	
1	2	0	0	÷100
		1	2	

Emphasise the movement of the digits two places to the right and, as a result, the loss of two zeros from any multiple of 100.

ACTIVITY 18.2

Resources
- 'The big divide' sheet on page 50

The big divide

On the board write a series of questions like the ones below.

| 80 ÷ 10 = | 60 ÷ 10 = | 90 ÷ 10 = | 70 ÷ 10 = |
| 800 ÷ 10 = | 600 ÷ 10 = | 900 ÷ 10 = | 700 ÷ 10 = |

Ask the children for the answers and the strategy they are using, which may be to remove a zero from the number to be divided, so 80 ÷ 10 = 8. (It is important that children see this as simply the *effect* of the digits moving to the right, otherwise problems are likely to occur when dividing decimals. For example, 7·30 does not become 7·3 when we divide by 10.)

Continue the activity by dividing by 100, the *effect* of which in these questions is the removal of two zeros.

800 ÷ 100 =   600 ÷ 100 =   900 ÷ 100 =   700 ÷ 100 =

The sheet on page 50 can be used to practise this work. Discuss patterns in the answers to consolidate these ideas.

PART III   DIVISION

Name ....

The big divide

18.2

Work these out in your head and write down the answers. Draw a line to join any questions that give the same answer. One has been done for you.

1) 50 ÷ 10 = 5
2) 60 ÷ 10 = ...
3) 90 ÷ 10 = ...

4) 500 ÷ 10 = ...
5) 600 ÷ 10 = ...
6) 900 ÷ 10 = ...

7) 5000 ÷ 10 = ...
8) 6000 ÷ 10 = ...
9) 9000 ÷ 10 = ...

10) 500 ÷ 100 = 5
11) 600 ÷ 100 = ...
12) 900 ÷ 100 = ...

13) 5000 ÷ 100 = ...
14) 6000 ÷ 100 = ...
15) 9000 ÷ 100 = ...

16) 50 000 ÷ 100 = ...
17) 60 000 ÷ 100 = ...
18) 90 000 ÷ 100 = ...

Here are the answers to some division questions.
Write some questions that give these answers. The first one is done for you.

19) 800 ÷ 10 = 80
20) .... ÷ .... = 90
21) .... ÷ .... = 18

22) .... ÷ .... = 30
23) .... ÷ .... = 200
24) .... ÷ .... = 190

25) .... ÷ .... = 300
26) .... ÷ .... = 10
27) .... ÷ .... = 34

19 Can divide any number by 10, 100, 1000 mentally

For example, 120 ÷ 10, 3000 ÷ 100, 98 ÷ 10, 27 530 ÷ 1000

ACTIVITY 19.1

Resources
- resource sheet 3 on page 60

Hurdles race 2

On the board draw four horizontal rows to represent race tracks, as shown. Mark on vertical dotted lines to represent 'hurdles'. Write the column headings above each column as shown.

M	HTh	TTh	Th	H	T	U	t	h
						7		
						9		
						3		
						8		

Split the class into four groups and explain that each group is taking part in a race. The aim is to move a single digit across from the units column to the millions column. Each group can choose a digit for their team. Write these digits into the units column, one in each row. A child from each group takes it in turns to choose one of the six cards marked ×10, ×100, ×1000, ÷10, ÷100, and ÷1000. (A team cannot begin if they select ÷1000 first.) Their digit then moves the appropriate number of columns across and zeros are written in the columns remaining. From this point on, if a move is possible, either multiplication or division, their digit moves as appropriate. The winning team is the one with the digit that reaches the millions column first.

The game can be played beginning with 2-digit numbers, and the thousandth column can also be introduced.

ACTIVITY 19.2

Resources
- resource sheet 3 on page 60
- calculator

In the circle

Sit the group in a circle, with one child in the centre holding the cards and a calculator. Choose a start number, such as 300 or 30, and give this to a child. The centre child turns up a card at random, for example, ×10, and the child given the number calculates the answer. The new number, the answer, passes to the child on the left and play continues. If the answer is wrong or the child is unable to answer, play passes to the left. The calculator can be used to check answers.

ACTIVITY 19.3

Resources
- 'On the move!' sheet on page 52
- calculator

On the move!

This activity begins by revisiting dividing by 10 before dividing whole numbers by 100. All answers are whole numbers. Column headings are initially emphasised and should be used by children in their written recording. A calculator can be used for checking.

ACTIVITY 19.4

Resources
- 'More moves!' sheet on page 53
- calculator

More moves!

This activity begins by revisiting dividing by 10 before moving on to dividing whole numbers and decimal numbers by 100. Answers are usually decimal numbers. Column headings are initially emphasised and should be used by children in their written recording. A calculator can be used for checking.

PART III DIVISION

(19.3)

Name

On the move!

Use a calculator to see what happens when you divide these numbers by 10. Write the answer underneath each one.
What do you notice? See if you can work out any without using a calculator.
As each digit becomes ten times smaller they appear to move! For example, 20 ÷ 10 = 2 and the '2' moves over into the units column and so on.

÷ 10

Th	H	T	U
		2	0
	2	3	0
3	5	0	0

Now try dividing these numbers by 100. How many places do the digits move and in which direction?

....

....

÷ 100

TTh	Th	H	T	U
		3	0	0
	6	0	0	0
	2	6	0	0
5	1	7	0	0
4	0	0	0	0

Fill in the missing numbers in the tables below.

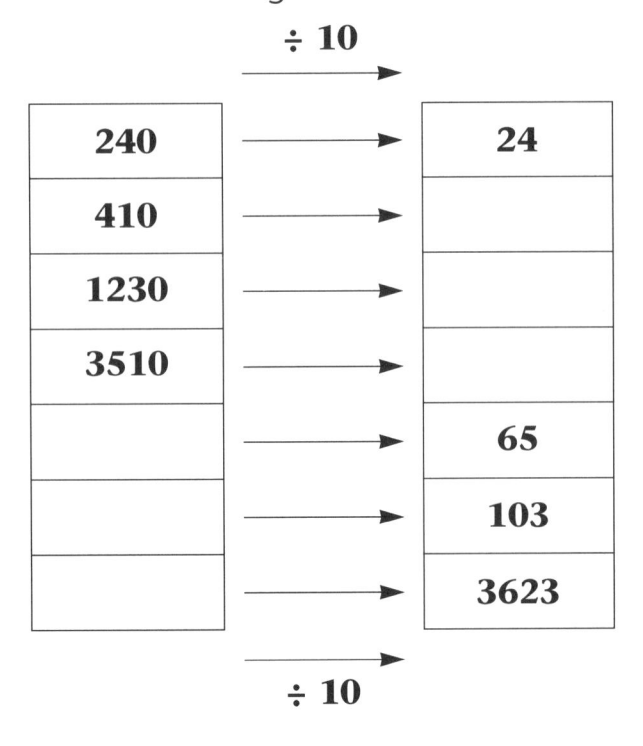

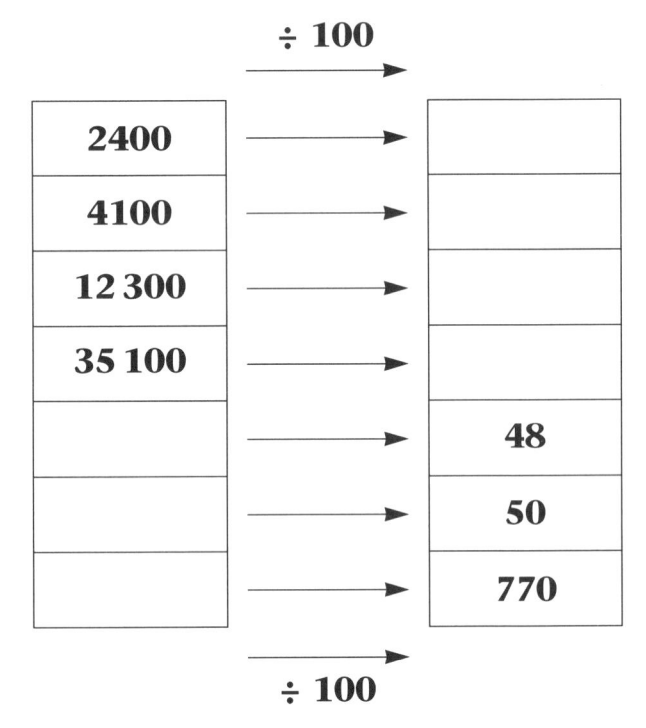

÷ 10 →

240	→	24
410	→	
1230	→	
3510	→	
	→	65
	→	103
	→	3623

← ÷ 10

÷ 100 →

2400	→	
4100	→	
12 300	→	
35 100	→	
	→	48
	→	50
	→	770

← ÷ 100

52 KS2 Numeracy Pack © Letts Educational, 1999

More moves!

Use a calculator to see what happens when you divide these numbers by 10. Write the answer underneath each one.
What do you notice? See if you can work out any without using a calculator.
As each digit becomes ten times smaller they appear to move! For example, 20 ÷ 10 = 2 and the '2' moves over into the units column and so on.

÷ 10

Th	H	T	U · t
		2	0
	2	3	7 ·
	5	0	6 ·

Now try dividing these numbers by 100. How many places do the digits move and in which direction?

....

....

÷ 100

Th	H	T	U · t	h
	8	0	0 ·	
6	0	0	0 ·	
2	6	1	0 ·	
5	1	0	8 ·	
4	0	5	2 ·	

Fill in the missing numbers in the tables below.

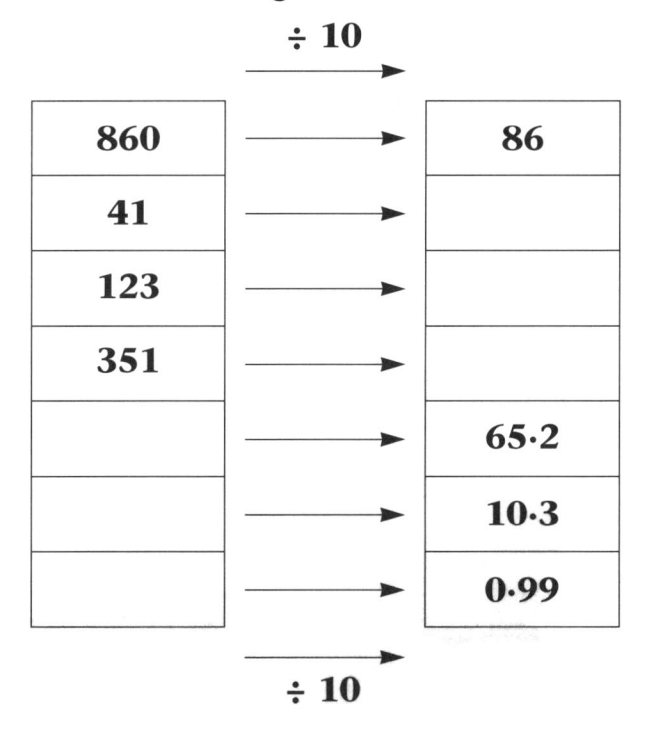

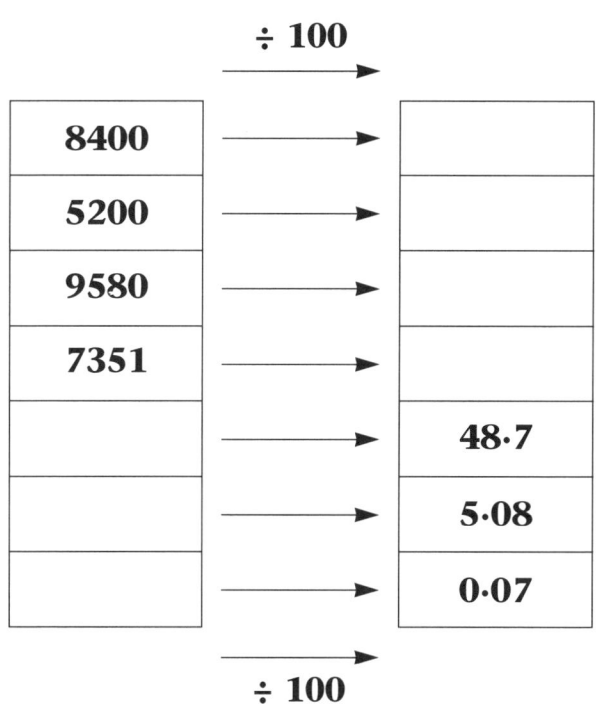

÷ 10 →

860	→	86
41	→	
123	→	
351	→	
	→	65·2
	→	10·3
	→	0·99

← ÷ 10

÷ 100 →

8400	→	
5200	→	
9580	→	
7351	→	
	→	48·7
	→	5·08
	→	0·07

← ÷ 100

PART III   DIVISION

20. Can divide a multiple of 100, 1000 by a multiple of 10, 100 mentally

For example, 600 ÷ 20, 800 ÷ 40, 1000 ÷ 20, 5000 ÷ 200

ACTIVITY 20.1

Resources
- none

Finding roots

Once children are comfortable with dividing any number by 10 we can help them to use this skill as a basis for dividing a multiple of 100 or 1000 by a multiple of 10 or 100.

On the board write a series of questions like the ones below to remind children of the strategies for dividing multiples of ten by ten.

    80 ÷ 10 =   60 ÷ 10 =   90 ÷ 10 =   70 ÷ 10 =

This may consist of removing a zero from the number to be divided, so 80 ÷ 10 = 8. (It is important that children see this as simply the *effect* of the digits moving to the right, otherwise problems are likely to occur when dividing decimals. For example, 7·30 does not become 7·3 when we divide by 10.)

Similarly, remind children of the strategies for dividing multiples of 100 by 10 or 100, which, in the latter case, may involve removing two zeros, as in 800 ÷ 100 = 8.

    800 ÷ 100 =   600 ÷ 100 =   900 ÷ 100 =   700 ÷ 100 =

Now extend these ideas by introducing divisors which are not 10 or 100 but are multiples of them.

    80 ÷ 20 =   60 ÷ 20 =   100 ÷ 20 =   140 ÷ 20 =

Encourage the continued use of previous strategies, so, for example, 80 ÷ 20 can be thought of as 8 ÷ 2.

Continue this with a range of divisors.

    90 ÷ 30 =   120 ÷ 40 =   200 ÷ 50 =   360 ÷ 60 =

Activity 20.2, 'Which way?' can be used to practise this work. Discuss patterns in the answers to consolidate these ideas.

ACTIVITY 20.2

Resources
- 'Which way?' sheet on page 55

Which way?

This sheet involves children mentally calculating the answers to simple questions to find a route around the roundabouts. As a child calculates an answer at a roundabout, the route showing the correct answer is followed to get to another roundabout. This is continued until a final destination is reached. The children have to discover which destination this is.

20 CAN DIVIDE A MULTIPLE OF 100, 1000 BY A MULTIPLE OF 10, 100 MENTALLY

20.2

Name

Which way?

Move to the first roundabout and answer the question. Follow the road with the correct answer to the next roundabout. Continue working out the answers and moving along the correct road. Where do you end up?

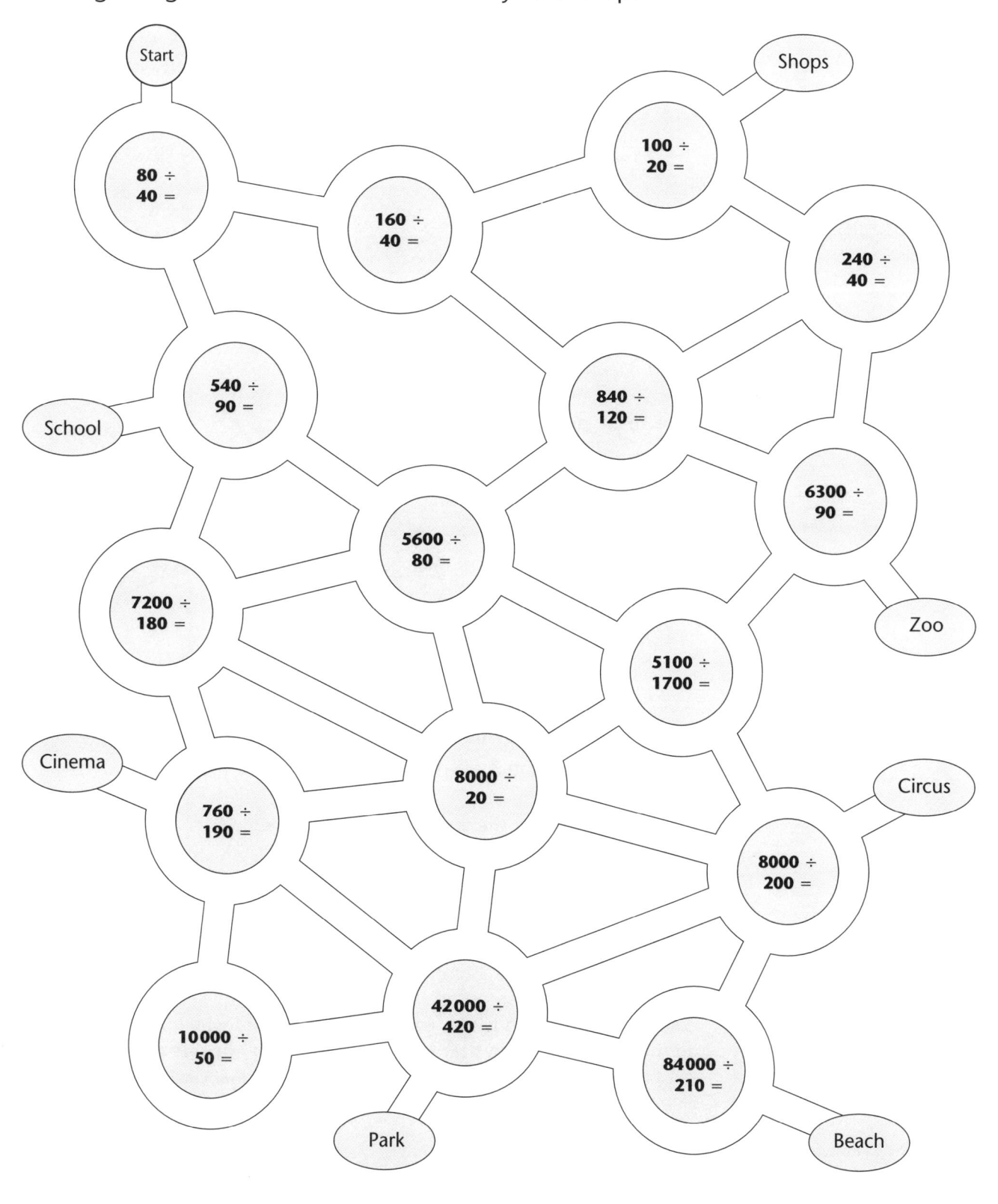

Start

Shops

80 ÷ 40 =

100 ÷ 20 =

160 ÷ 40 =

240 ÷ 40 =

School

540 ÷ 90 =

840 ÷ 120 =

6300 ÷ 90 =

5600 ÷ 80 =

7200 ÷ 180 =

Zoo

5100 ÷ 1700 =

Cinema

8000 ÷ 20 =

Circus

760 ÷ 190 =

8000 ÷ 200 =

42000 ÷ 420 =

10000 ÷ 50 =

84000 ÷ 210 =

Park

Beach

KS2 Numeracy Pack © Letts Educational, 1999

55

PART III DIVISION

21. Can divide a single digit by a larger single digit giving a fractional or decimal answer mentally

For example, 1 ÷ 2, 1 ÷ 4, 3 ÷ 4, 4 ÷ 5, 6 ÷ 8

ACTIVITY 21.1

Resources
- none

Divide and conquer!

On the board, draw three circles and explain that these are three large cakes. If there were 5 children, how much would each child get, if the cakes were equally shared? Write this question as a division question, i.e. 3 ÷ 5 =   .

Invite children to attempt to divide the three cakes into 5 *equal* sections. Many attempts may be necessary, as children find difficulty in partitioning equally.

After some time, if children haven't already discovered the following as a strategy, introduce it: What if we split each cake into 5 equal pieces?

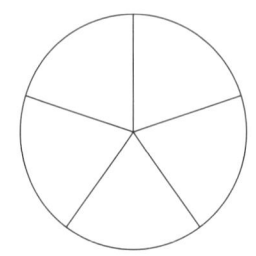

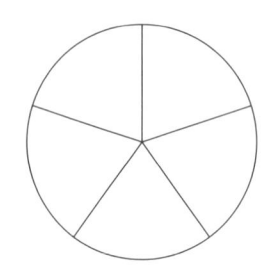

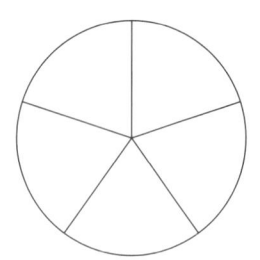

How many pieces would each child get now?

Colour in the 3 fifths of the cakes in different colours, as below.

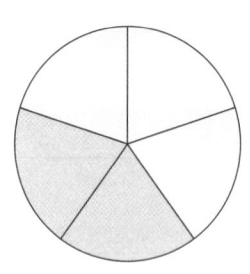

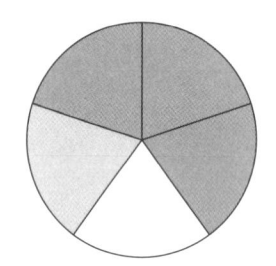

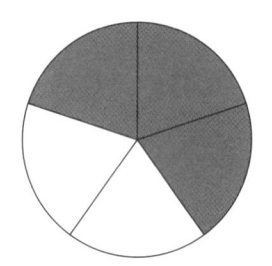

How would we write this amount as a fraction of one cake ($\frac{3}{5}$)?

Rewrite the question 3 ÷ 5 next to this answer. Do the children notice anything?

What do they think the answer to 2 ÷ 5 will be?

Encourage them to see the pattern between division and fractions.

ACTIVITY 21.2

Resources
- 'The last circuits! cards' on page 57

The last circuits!

Use the cards on page 57 for this activity. Give one card to each child and read the question on one card aloud, for example, 'One divided by four is…?'. One child in the group will have a card which has the answer to the question, which they call out, followed by the question on their card. Play continues until the answer on the original card is reached.

21 CAN DIVIDE A SINGLE DIGIT BY A LARGER SINGLE DIGIT GIVING A FRACTIONAL OR DECIMAL ANSWER MENTALLY

21.2

The last circuits! cards

0·25	**0·5**	**0·8**	**0·2**
1 ÷ 2 =	4 ÷ 5 =	1 ÷ 5 =	3 ÷ 4 =
0·75	**0·75**	**0·5**	**0·25**
6 ÷ 8 =	3 ÷ 6 =	1 ÷ 4 =	2 ÷ 8 =
$\frac{1}{4}$	$\frac{1}{2}$	$\frac{4}{5}$	$\frac{1}{5}$
1 ÷ 2 =	4 ÷ 5 =	1 ÷ 5 =	3 ÷ 4 =
$\frac{3}{4}$	$\frac{3}{4}$	$\frac{1}{2}$	$\frac{1}{4}$
6 ÷ 8 =	3 ÷ 6 =	1 ÷ 4 =	2 ÷ 8 =

KS2 Numeracy Pack © Letts Educational, 1999

RESOURCE SHEETS

Number generator

R1

This sheet of numbers can be used for oral questioning, to ensure that a broad range of numbers, including simple fractions and decimals, is used. Select randomly from these numbers when generating questions, such as 'What is 10 multiplied by...?', 'If a .... costs £..., how much will 99 of them cost?', etc.

1 2 3 4 5 6 7 8 9 10 11 12 13 14 15 16 17 18 19 20

30 40 50 60 70 80 90 100 110 120 130 140 150 160 170 180 190 200

11 22 33 44 55 66 77 88 99   25 35 45 65 75 85 95

24 26 28 32 34 36 38 42 46 48 52 54 56 58 62 64 68 72 74 76 78 82 84 86 92 94 96 98

21 23 27 29 31 37 39 41 43 47 49 51 53 57 59 61 63 67 69 71 73 79 81 83 87 89 91 93 97

200 300 400 500 600 700 800 900 1000   250 350 450 550 650 750 850 950

222   444   666   888   848   884   882   868   864   862   826   824   688   686
646   626   624   644   662   664   488   484   486   468   442   446   448   248
288   244   266   264   246...

220 240 260 280 320 340 360 380 420 440 460 480 520 540 560 580 620 640 660 680 720 740 760 780 820 840 860 880 920 940 960 980

101 201 301 401 501 601 701 801 901 199 299 399 499 599 699 799 899 999

$\frac{1}{2}$ $\frac{1}{4}\frac{2}{4}\frac{3}{4}$ $\frac{1}{8}\frac{2}{8}\frac{3}{8}\frac{4}{8}\frac{5}{8}\frac{6}{8}\frac{7}{8}$ $\frac{1}{3}\frac{2}{3}$ $\frac{1}{6}\frac{2}{6}\frac{3}{6}\frac{4}{6}\frac{5}{6}$ $\frac{1}{5}\frac{2}{5}\frac{3}{5}\frac{4}{5}$

$\frac{1}{10}\frac{2}{10}\frac{3}{10}\frac{5}{10}\frac{9}{10}$ $\frac{1}{100}\frac{3}{100}\frac{50}{100}\frac{25}{100}\frac{75}{100}$ $\frac{1}{16}\frac{4}{16}$ $\frac{1}{20}\frac{5}{20}$ $\frac{1}{32}\frac{4}{32}$ ...

0·5   0·25   0·75   0·1   0·2   0·3   0·4   0·5   0·6   0·7   0·8   0·9

1·2   1·4   1·6   1·8   2·2   2·4   2·6   2·8   3·2   3·4   3·6   3·8   4·2   4·4
4·6   4·8   5·2   5·4   5·6   5·8   6·2   6·4   6·6   6·8   7·2   7·4   7·6   7·8
8·2   8·4   8·6   8·8   9·2   9·4   9·6   9·8

8·88 6·66 4·44 2·22 0·88 0·66 0·44 0·22 8·66 8·44 8·22 6·44 6·22 4·66 4·22 4·88

0·12   0·14   0·16   0·18   0·24   0·26   0·28   0·32   0·34   0·36   0·38   0·42   0·46   0·48
0·52   0·54   0·56   0·58   0·62   0·64   0·68   0·72   0·74   0·76   0·78   0·82   0·84   0·86
0·92   0·94   0·96   0·98

1200 1300 1400 1500 1600 1700 1800 1900 2200 2500 4200 7500

1000 2000 3000 4000 5000 6000 7000 8000 9000 10 000 20 000 30 000...

0–9 cards

1	2	3	4
5	6	7	8
9	0	1	2
3	4	5	6
7	8	9	0

One step stepping

$\times 10$	$\div 10$
$\times 100$	$\div 100$
$\times 1000$	$\div 1000$

Answers

PART I   COMPETENCIES FOR MULTIPLICATION AND DIVISION

5) Understands place value ideas and can partition numbers, and understands relationships between single- and 2- and 3-digit numbers

5.2 Spot the pattern!

(1) 4   8   16
     40   80   160
     400   800   1600

(2) 4   8   16
     40   80   160
     400   800   1600

(3) 20   21   36
     2000   2100   3600

(4) 16   160   1600   160   1600
     12   120   1200   120   1200
     45   450   4500   450   4500
     28   280   2800   280   2800
     4000   400   40   4
     8000   800   80   8

PART II   MULTIPLICATION

7) Can multiply any number by 10 mentally

7.2 Machine madness!

(1) 40   650   730   990
(2) 2300   6700   5030   6090
(3) 8   13   45   74
(4) 125   237   619   972
(5) 500   700   900   1000
(6) 3300   4500   5080   7070

7.3 Birthday treats!

(1) Ice-cream
(2) Milk
(3) 10
(4) £9.90
(5) £11.20
(6) £7.50
(7) £27.00
(9) £6.70
(10) £4.60
(11) £5.00
(12) 10
(13) 10

8) Can multiply any number by 9 or 11 mentally

8.3 Doing the shopping

(1) £3.52   £2.88
(2) £19.25   £15.75
(3) £4.62   £3.78
(4) £4.07   £3.33
(5) £10.89   £8.91   £21.78   £17.82
(6) £8.25   £6.75   £16.50   £13.50

8.4 More birthday treats!

(1) Ice-cream
(2) Milk
(3) £10.89
(4) £8.91
(5) £12.76
(6) £10.44
(7) £8.58
(8) £7.02
(9) £30.25   £24.75
(10) £7.59
(11) £4.14
(12) £5.50
(13) 11

61

ANSWERS

9) Can multiply any number by 100 mentally

9.2 Making a move

540	1590	6071				
6500	4000	93 230	33 080	70 700		
41	5320	95·3	753	10·3	9·9	
7500	870	99 800	351	86·8	9·04	70

9.3 Snowballing

3	30	3000	30 000	3 000 000
5	50	5000	50 000	5 000 000
12	120	12 000	120 000	12 000 000
6	600	60 000	6 000 000	
23	2300	230 000	23 000 000	
4·2	420	42 000	4 200 000	
14·7	1470	147 000	14 700 000	

10) Can multiply any number by 99 or 101, etc. mentally

10.4 Cook's maths

(**1**) £5.05   £4.95   (**4**) £37.37   £36.63

(**2**) £17.17 £16.83   (**5**) £20.20   £19.80
                                £40.40   £39.60

(**3**) £42.42 £41.58

11) Can multiply any number by 1000 mentally

11.3 Moving!

650	4070			
3800	26 100	71 000		
2000	46 000	328 000	502 000	300 000
10 300	523 400	73	650	
29 000	531 000	460 000	34	48

11.4 Moving with decimals

350	5172					
9800	6070	66 930				
2000	4600	328 400	502 700	300 000		
290	839	652·1	65·2	6·03	0·68	
2800	8500	8390	6520	48·7	6·008	0·6

12) Can multiply any number by 999 or 1001, etc. mentally

12.4 At the match

(**1**) £400.40   £399.60   (**4**) £370.37   £369.63

(**2**) £850.85   £849.15   (**5**) £200.20   £199.80   £400.40   £399.60

(**3**) £420.42   £419.58

13) Can multiply two multiples of 10, 100, 1000 mentally

13.3 How many zeros?

(**1**) 150   (**2**) 1500   (**3**) 15 000   (**4**) 150   (**5**) 1500
(**6**) 15 000   (**7**) 1500   (**8**) 15 000   (**9**) 150 000   (**10**) 280
(**11**) 2800   (**12**) 28 000   (**13**) 280   (**14**) 2800   (**15**) 28 000
(**16**) 2800   (**17**) 28 000   (**18**) 280 000   (**19**) 540   (**20**) 5400
(**21**) 54 000   (**22**) 540   (**23**) 5400   (**24**) 54 000   (**25**) 5400
(**26**) 54 000   (**27**) 540 000   (**28**) 540 000   (**29**) 5 400 000 (**30**) 54 000 000

ANSWERS

PART III DIVISION

17) Can divide a 2-digit number by a single digit without or with remainders mentally

17.1 Head it!

(1) 11   (2) 17   (3) 16   (4) 12   (5) 18
(6) 11   (7) 12   (8) 11   (9) 13   (10) 37
(11) 15   (12) 14   (13) 16 r 4   (14) 30 r 2   (15) 15 r 2

18) Can divide a multiple of 10 by 10, and a multiple of 100 by 10 or 100 mentally

18.2 The big divide

(1) 5   (2) 6   (3) 9   (4) 50   (5) 60
(6) 90   (7) 500   (8) 600   (9) 900   (10) 5
(11) 6   (12) 9   (13) 50   (14) 60   (15) 90
(16) 500 (17) 600 (18) 900

19) Can divide any number by 10, 100, 1000 mentally

19.3 On the move!

2	23	350				
3	60	26	517	400		
41	123	351	650	1030	36 230	
24	41	123	351	4800	5000	77 000

19.4 More moves!

2	23·7	50·6				
8	60	26·1	51·08	40·52		
4·1	12·3	35·1	652	103	9·9	
84	52	95·8	73·51	4870	508	7

20) Can divide a multiple of 100, 1000 by a multiple of 10, 100 mentally

20.2 Which way?

The zoo

63